Theatre in Practice

Theatre in Practice provides students with all of the 'must have' drama skills required for A level, International Baccalaureate, BTEC and beyond. Practical, step-by-step exercises and diagrams give access to the key figures and processes central to drama, including:

- Stanislavski, Brecht, Lecoq and Berkoff
- devising theatre
- rehearsing and performing monologues and duologues
- how to approach directing a play
- improvising.

Each chapter offers advice for both students and teachers, with notes and follow-on exercises ideal for individual study and practice. Written by specialists with extensive experience leading workshops for the 'post-16' age group, *Theatre in Practice* is a thorough and imaginative resource that speaks directly to students.

Nick O'Brien trained as an Actor and Director for four years under Sam Kogan, who was a pupil of Maria Knebel, one of Stanislavski's pupils at the Moscow Art Theatre. He has a PGCE in Drama from Keele University. Nick taught Stanislavski-based Acting Technique at Excel School of Performing Arts and B.S.A. He is Head of Drama at the New London Performing Arts Centre and has worked for Edexcel for a number of years as an examiner and moderator. Nick founded and runs the Stanislavski Experience, a drama workshop company. He is the author of *Stanislavski in Practice*, also published by Routledge.

Annie Sutton trained with Desmond Jones at his School of Mime and Physical Theatre and at École Jacques Lecoq. She has a PGCE (distinction) in Film and Drama. Annie is a theatre maker and currently leads projects for Hornchurch Queen's Theatre. She has worked for Hampstead Theatre, The Royal Court Theatre, the Globe, Theatre Centre, Unicorn and Cheltenham Literature Festival as a freelance practitioner.

Theatre in Practice

A student's handbook

NICK O'BRIEN
ANNIE SUTTON

Illustrations by Mayumi Ogiwara
Photography by Matt Cooper

 Routledge
Taylor & Francis Group

LONDON AND NEW YORK

First published 2013
by Routledge
2 Park Square, Milton Park, Abingdon, Oxon OX14 4RN

Simultaneously published in the USA and Canada
by Routledge
711 Third Avenue, New York, NY 10017

Routledge is an imprint of the Taylor & Francis Group, an informa business

© 2013 Nick O'Brien and Annie Sutton
Illustrations © 2013 Mayumi Ogiwari
Photographs © 2013 Matt Cooper

The right of Nick O'Brien and Annie Sutton to be identified as the authors
of this work has been asserted by them in accordance with sections 77 and
78 of the Copyright, Designs and Patents Act 1988.

British Library Cataloguing in Publication Data
A catalogue record for this book is available from the British Library

Library of Congress Cataloging-in-Publication Data
A catalog record for this title has been requested

ISBN: 978-0-415-50853-7 (pbk)
ISBN: 978-0-203-12542-7 (ebk)

Typeset in Charter ITC and Folio
by Florence Production Ltd, Stoodleigh, Devon, UK

Printed and bound by CPI Group (UK) Ltd, Croydon, CR0 4YY

FOR YULI

FOR PORKY SUTTON

Contents

Figures

Tables

Acknowledgements

Many thanks go to Mayumi Ogiwara for producing another series of excellent illustrations and to Matt Cooper for his wonderful photography. To Thomas Conway for his help with Chapter 6 on devising theatre, Tom has given a wealth of feedback and ideas that have helped to give the chapter its Artaudian feel.

Thanks to Michaela Brooks, Millie Burgh, Hannah Carson and Amy Cotter for all their help with the photos for this book and to NLPAC for the use of the studio space. Thanks to Michelle Blair at CPA studios and Katriona Brown, Samuel Hopkins, Joseph O Reilly, Shelley Payne, Kristian Turner and Emma White for participating in the Lecoq/Berkoff workshops.

Many thanks to Talia Rodgers, Ben Piggott and Sam Kinchin-Smith for all their help in transforming an idea into reality.

Thanks also to all the teachers and students that have had 'the Stanislavski Experience'. This book is very much a product of our work in your studios across the country and would have been impossible without you!

Finally, thanks to Nick's wife, Yuli, and his children, Marcus and Lillia, for putting up with him while he put pen to paper.

Annie's thanks also go to Desmond Jones and Tom Wilde for giving her the discipline, to Joff Chafer, Robert Daniels, Fraser Hooper and Yasmin Gurreeboo for their inspiration, William Ilkley and the family Georgiakis for their Greek collaborations, to all sumo warriors, and to David and Beryl Kennedy. Special thanks to Steven Berkoff. Finally to Dave Snell and Di Sutton for their love.

The author and the publishers would like to thank the following for their kind permission: A&C Black/Bloomsbury for the rights to use extracts from Bertolt Brecht's *The Caucasian Chalk Circle*, translated by James and Tania Stern with W. H. Auden.

Introduction

BEFORE YOU START

This book is not the kind of book you read and then put down; this is more of a 'read and then give it a go' book.

Acting is about doing and so this book is designed for you to work through and practise a series of different exercises. The best way to understand theatre, acting and the ideas of the key practitioners is by practising them.

With this in mind, this book is a series of exercises that will help you to understand what acting is and the ideas of the leading theatre practitioners. So if you read an exercise then give that exercise a go straight away, or if you have worked through an exercise in class then go away and practise the follow-on exercise at home.

In this book you will hear two different voices. For the majority of the book you will hear my voice – Nick O'Brien. I will be the voice of Chapter 1 on Stanislavski, Chapter 2 on Brecht, Chapter 5 on rehearsing a monologue/duologue, Chapter 6 on devising theatre, Chapter 7 on improvising with a practitioner and Chapter 8 on directing a play. You will hear Annie Sutton's voice in Chapter 3 on Lecoq and Chapter 4 on Berkoff. Annie is a wonderful physical theatre practitioner. Annie and I have run a number of workshops together where I will do 2 hours of Stanislavski and then, after a break, she will run 2 hours of Lecoq/Berkoff while I sit back, drink coffee and marvel at the creative work she immerses the group in.

You can use this book in different ways. You can start at Stanislavski and work through all the exercises on the system then move on to the other three main practitioners, or you may, in relation to what you are doing in class, focus on one or two practitioners in particular. The second section of the book focuses on rehearsing a monologue and duologue, devising a piece of original theatre and directing a play, which will help you gain the key skills you need at post-16. Throughout this book, there will be notes for the students and the teacher. If you are a student, you can skip the italicised notes for the teacher and just read the notes for the student.

Recently, I had a new student come to me at the end of a LAMDA examination lesson. She was working towards her silver medallion and said to me, 'I read the chapter on actions in your *Stanislavski in Practice* book and I don't get it'. So I asked her if she had tried to do the exercises, but she told me that she had just read it! I told her to go away and practise the exercises in the chapter and then we could talk. The next week, she turned up with a bashful look and before I could say anything she smiled and said, 'Yeah, yeah I get it now'. It reminded me how important actually doing an exercise is. As with all the exercises in this book, just reading them will never work; it is the getting up and doing them that will produce results.

WHERE THE IDEAS AND EXERCISES IN THIS BOOK CAME FROM

Annie Sutton and I work for the Stanislavski Experience. We visit schools, colleges and universities running workshops on our specialised areas. These workshops are practical ways into understanding a practitioner or delivering the skills to devise or work on a monologue/duologue. We run workshops throughout the UK with the purpose of allowing students to experience and understand through practice.

This book and the exercises in it are ones that have been tried and tested in schools and colleges across the country and are proven to work. Many of the exercises are Stanislavski's or Brecht's or Lecoq's own that have been shaped and developed to best suit the post-16 Drama student.

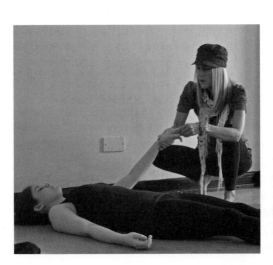

Figure i.1
Annie Sutton

Figure i.2
Nick O'Brien

The exercises within each chapter are designed to allow you, the student, to experience and understand the various processes of acting so you have a clear knowledge based on practical application.

Some of the exercises you may well recognise and have experienced before under a different name, as, over the years, exercises and ideas have been developed and 'made their own' by each new practitioner. I often smile as I am told about a new experimental exercise that is simply a variation on an exercise that was used by Stanislavski over 100 years ago in the studios of the Moscow Art Theatre.

Each chapter is what we feel works best in the studio on a given practitioner and, in many cases, is ideal for the post-16 student or first year undergraduate to gain a clear, solid understanding of a practitioner's work.

HOW TO USE THE BOOK

For the student

For each chapter, simply start at the beginning and work through the exercises. As you go, you will get a greater understanding of the practitioner involved. The majority of exercises are student exercises that you can work on as a group or alone, with follow-on exercises for you to work on at home. There are also teacher-led exercises for your teacher or group leader to work through with you.

The first four chapters will start with Stanislavski before moving on to Brecht, Lecoq and Berkoff. The first part of each chapter will be comprised of exercises that help you to understand that practitioner and give you some key skills to use. The next section of each chapter will look at how you use that practitioner when working on a text or when devising a piece of theatre. Each chapter will be slightly different depending on the practitioner it serves. For those of you on A level, BTEC or IB courses, this will cover the bases you need for your practical work and give you grounding in the theory. The end of each chapter summarises the key ideas and practices so you have a clear understanding of the areas you have experienced and learnt. For those of you on undergraduate courses, whether in the US, the UK or else-where, this book will give you a quick, practical recap that will allow you to move on to exploring the practitioners in greater depth.

A number of the exercises can be done in class as a group or in multiple groups, with follow-on exercises that you can practise at home. It is always a good idea to evaluate each exercise after you have done it, and you can read over the notes for the student to help clarify any questions you may have.

With each practitioner comes a specific language often unique to that practitioner. Every time we use a new acting term, it will be written in **bold**, and you will find a definition for it in the margin and in the glossary towards the back of the book (see page 233).

There is also a further reading section at the back of the book to point you in the direction of the practitioners' own works and other useful material to help you (see page 242).

Chapters 5, 6 and 8 are step-by-step approaches to working on a monologue/duologue, devising a piece of theatre and directing a play. These chapters are designed to take you from start to finish, guaranteeing you a solid base and structure from which to be creative! Chapter 6 includes a section that explores devising from Artaud's perspective, with exercises designed to help you create a devised piece using his ideas. Chapter 7 is full of improvisation to work on individually, in pairs and in groups, and is set up for you to use in conjunction with the practitioners that you have already explored.

In a book of this nature, not everything can be covered; so, for example, in Chapter 1 on Stanislavski, the exercises you encounter serve as a practical summary of the key workings of the system. For a more in-depth look, you can refer to books such as *Stanislavski in Practice* or Stanislavski's *An Actor's Work*, both listed in the further reading section.

Many of you reading this book will be about to embark on any number of drama and theatre courses. In class, you may be working on practitioners not featured in this book or you may only glance at these seminal practitioners before looking at more contemporary ones. For you, as students, it is of real importance that you have a solid grounding in the key ideas of theatre, so, with this book in hand, you will be secure in the knowledge that you covered the key ideas on which modern theatre practice is based.

For the teacher

It is always worth reminding yourself that we do not learn how to act or how to understand a practitioner simply by being told something. We learn through doing something, experiencing and then evaluating. That is what this book is all about; it looks at a range of key practitioners with a series of exercises for students to explore and experience. Each chapter ends with a summary box of the key elements of the practice and theory explored in that chapter.

Stanislavski's students were not given a copy of his book to read; they were guided through a series of exercises that helped them to understand the system. Brecht got his actors up on their feet, working and exploring, and Lecoq did the same. This book will give students a full practical understanding of a practitioner that will put them in the ideal position to then explore the practitioner's own works. In that way, you can best recreate how that practitioner would have worked and give students the best path to understanding.

Introducing students to a practitioner through a series of exercises will lead them to a practical understanding of how to put any theory into context.

Acting theory is really just an understanding of the practical. Once students have understood in practice, taking a theoretical viewpoint will come easily to them.

I have been into schools and colleges where teachers have used my first book, Stanislavski in Practice, *in different ways. Some have read an exercise themselves and then run the exercise with the group. Others have given each student a book and, in groups, they have worked through an exercise, shown the results and then evaluated as a class. The teacher has then sent them off to work on the follow-on exercise at home to then show in the next class. I have been told that using this method allows teachers to observe and assess their students at work, watching them experience, explore and solve problems as a group.*

Within this book, I have chosen four key practitioners in the first section and have given the devising chapter a practitioner focus. For AS and A2 courses where you need to examine text in the light of a practitioner, you can choose from one of these four and, when students are devising using a practitioner, they can use Chapters 1–4 on the practitioners and Chapter 6 on devising theatre. Many schools introduce specific practitioners at KS3 and KS4, so you can dip into this book to give you ideas on how to structure your schemes of work.

Chapter 5 on rehearsing a monologue/duologue gives the students a structure through which to work in order to research, rehearse and show their monologue. This means that you can give them a clear structure to guide them through the process. Chapter 6 on devising theatre does the same with devising a piece of theatre, giving the students exercises to help them create and focus their time. Chapter 7 on improvising with a practitioner gives you the opportunity to watch students working on set improvisations, allowing you to evaluate their progress on a given practitioner and see how much has sunk in. Chapter 8 on directing a play is, in many ways, the teacher-director's chapter to help with directing a play. When you are directing, it provides a simple step-by-step guide to refer to, with exercises to help you engage with the text you are working on and structure your rehearsal times.

As teachers working within the current specifications, you have the opportunity to choose which practitioners to focus on. A solid grounding in the key practitioners will always be the best option for students, but this is not always possible within the time constraints you have. With this book, you can send students off to research and work on a variety of practitioners and then report back, putting the onus on them to explore and experience and then show and evaluate their findings. For those of you wishing to explore more con-temporary practitioners, you can use the exercises in this book as grounding for your chosen practitioner's work, from which you can further explore their style. So, for Katie Mitchell, you use the exercises in Chapter 1 on Stanislavski and then use her style to suit the play you have chosen. Or, if you are exploring Complicite's style, you can use the exercises in Chapter 3 on Lecoq.

I am often surprised how much practical work students get through at home, often telling me of how they have run exercises with their mum, dad or girlfriend/boyfriend with interesting results.

I ran a workshop recently in a school with two large AS groups using Stanislavski as their chosen practitioner. I ran the first workshop and then, after lunch, met the second group. Halfway through the workshop, I introduced a communication exercise. One of the students put his hand up and said, 'is this the one where . . .' and described the exercise I was about to run exactly. I said it was and he said, 'Oh, we've all been doing that this lunchtime in the sixth form common room, the other group taught us'!

More often than not, the exercises do all the work for you. You give the students an exercise, step back and then guide and tweak, allowing them to experience, explore and evaluate. That is really what this book is for – I hope it helps!

To further help you to put these exercises into practice, the Stanislavski Experience will be holding teacher INSET days where you will be able to work with the authors and see the exercises in this book brought alive. For more information on booking a place on a 'Using Practitioners' INSET day, go to www.stanislavskiexp.co.uk.

AT WHAT LEVEL CAN I USE THIS BOOK?

This book caters for post-16 students at AS/A2 as well as BTEC and International Baccalaureate students. The chapters on the practitioners and the focus on rehearsing a monologue and duologue, devising and directing theatre fulfil a number of requirements across the various specifications at post-16.

If you are on an AS or A2 course, you could use Chapters 1–4 on the practitioners when working on a practitioner with a text and then Chapter 5 on devising theatre when creating a piece of devised theatre. A practical knowledge of the five practitioners in this book (Stanislavski, Brecht, Lecoq, Berkoff and Artaud) will help you across all four units and feed into:

- devising work in a chosen style;
- theatre review;
- performing and analysing text; and
- working from the director's perspective.

AS and A2 students who are using contemporary practitioners in their devised and text work will benefit greatly from a grounding in the key practitioners from whom the ideas of contemporary practitioners have grown.

For International Baccalaureate students, the book will help across all three units in Group 6 and can play a part in compiling your journal and your individual project. For students studying the new Literature and Performance in Group 1, the text sections of each practitioner will help in their work in transforming text into performance.

At BTEC, the exercises in this book will give you an armoury of tools to use across the mandatory and optional units from Principle of Acting to Rehearsing for Performance and Devising Plays, Mime and Developing Physical Theatre.

For students rehearsing for LAMDA exams, Chapter 5 on rehearsing a monologue/duologue will provide you with a structure to guide your rehearsals and give you a series of exercises to work on during and outside of class. This chapter also provides a structure for those applying for drama schools or requiring monologues for auditions.

University and drama school students will find Chapters 1–4 on the practitioners useful to give them a practical grounding of the key ideas in theatre and to provide a series of concrete exercises to do at home to support the work done in class.

Many students at GCSE today will work on the key practitioners, and teachers and students will find a number of exercises useful in both work on text and devising. GCSE groups that have to devise their own pieces will find Chapter 6 on devising theatre useful in giving a concrete structure to follow.

PART 1

Key practitioners

1 Stanislavski and the system (1889–1956)

Konstantin Stanislavski created a system. It was a system for acting that enables us, as actors, to create **truthful** and believable characters. Stanislavski's system is as vibrant a system for acting today as it was all those years ago in the studios and rehearsal rooms of the Moscow Art Theatre. Today, the system is still the most comprehensive acting method we have, and Stanislavski's ideas have dominated theatre for over 80 years.

Think of his system as a useful set of exercises to help you act better. It is not about trying to copy what Stanislavski would have done 100 years ago, but more a case of using his system to work on the character and play you have before you. It is about making the system your own so you can use it to be a better actor. You go through the exercises, practise them and then use them with a role and evaluate the results.

This chapter will work through the main areas of Stanislavski's system and then move on to using the system when working on a text. The key to understanding and using Stanislavski's system is to experience it practically, through a series of exercises, which is what we will be doing.

As you will see in this chapter, Stanislavski's system can be used with almost any text, from Chekhov's *The Seagull* to one of the National Theatre's New Connections plays.

For you, the student, Stanislavski is the best place to start your exploration of theatre practitioners. This chapter will give you a solid foundation on which to explore and experience the other practitioners in this book.

Today, the work of theatre director Katie Mitchell is a good example of how the system is now being used, and a number of the exercises in this chapter are the kind of exercises that Mitchell uses at the National Theatre and the Royal Court.

Read these words by Stanislavski now and decide what you think he meant. Then read them again after you have completed the exercises in this chapter. See if you have a better understanding of what Stanislavski wanted of you as an actor.

> Our purpose is not only to create 'the life of the human spirit in a role', but also to communicate it outwardly in an artistic form. So the actor

truthful
Acting is truthful when based on a set of given circumstances; you are thinking and doing as the character, imagining actively with a free body and a clear walk through before time.

must not only experience the role inwardly, he must embody that inner experience physically. Outer communication relies very strongly on inner experiencing in our school of acting. To be able to reflect a life which is subtle and often subconscious, you must possess an exceptionally responsive and outstandingly well trained voice and body, which must be able to convey hidden, almost imperceptible inner feelings instantly in a distinct and accurate manner.[1]

UNDERSTANDING STANISLAVSKI THROUGH PRACTICE: WORK ON THE ACTOR

1 IMAGINATION

Student exercise

AIM

To work on actively using your **imagination**.

imagination
The ability to treat fictional circumstances as if they were real.

- Find a space and stand in a relaxed position.
- Allow yourself to be gently pulled up by the strings. Imagine a piece of string running from the base of your spine through the top of your head and up to the ceiling. Imagine this string is being gently pulled and this will put you into the correct position to use your imagination.
- Imagine you are standing before a desert. You can see the dunes running off into the distance, you can hear the wind whipping up the sand and you can feel the sand blowing against your face. You can feel the sun beating down on to your face and a dry, dust-like sensation in your mouth.
- Now imagine you are standing at the edge of a waterfall. You can hear the deafening sound of the water crashing around you, you can feel the gentle spray of water on your face and hands, you can smell lavender wafting in the air.
- You are now standing in the middle of a field. It is the middle of the night and there is not a cloud in the sky. The stars cover the sky and the deadly silence is interrupted very occasionally by a far-off sound.

- Now imagine your kitchen at home. Using your imagination, place the objects around you. You can hear the hum of the fridge, the smell of recently made toast, the sound of a radio in the other room. Gently imagine all this and then bring in an impression of the rest of the house, where the rooms are, then imagine the garden and the road you live on.

Student follow-on exercise: the magic if

- Find a quiet space and sit down.
- Whatever the time is now, ask yourself what if it was 12 hours later. Start to think about how you would feel if it was now the middle of the night.
- Ask yourself: What if I was living in Russia, in Moscow? How would my life be different?
- Now imagine that you live in Moscow but the year is 1917 and revolution is all around you. Ask yourself: What if I was a student in Moscow and my country was on the outbreak of civil war? How would I feel and what would I be thinking?

Figure 1.1
Pulled up by the strings

Figure 1.2
Michaela is imagining standing before the desert with the sun on her face. When you look into her eyes, you see that she is imagining different surroundings to those she is currently in

magic if
The question 'what if' that an actor asks himself or herself to trigger the imagination within a given set of circumstances.

active imagination
Seeing things through our character's eyes using the five senses.

given circumstance
The situation the character is in within a particular bit of the play.

objective
What we, as the character, want to achieve within a given set of circumstances.

action
What we do, as the character, to fulfil our objective.

Questions for after the exercise

- Did using the **magic if** help to trigger your imagination?
- Did using the magic if help to create different pictures around you?
- When you used the magic if, did you find that, as your imagination started to work, this brought about a change in what you were thinking and feeling?

Notes for the student

Imagination is the actor's ability to treat fictional circumstances as if they were real. When we imagine, we need to use **active imagination**. So, what can we see, hear, touch, taste and smell as the character? You will need to use your imagination to create your character's past, the **given circumstances**, your character's future, your **objective** and **action**. It is your imagination that gels all the other areas of the system together and, as an actor, you need to practise using your imagination throughout your training and beyond. With this exercise, remember to relax and do not force your imagination. If you find it difficult to start with, do not force anything, but gently build using your imagination over a longer period of time rather than going for immediate results.

Acting tip

When acting, ask yourself: What if my character was in that circumstance? What would I be thinking and doing?

2 CREATING PICTURES AND IMPRESSIONS

Student exercise

AIM

To harness the imagination to create active pictures and impressions.

- Go for a walk on your own, ideally in the country, a forest or a park. Try to find somewhere away from other people.

- As you are walking, use your imagination to create pictures and impressions of the following character's life:
  You are 26 and work as a runner for a large record label in Soho, London. You live with two friends in a flat in Clapham, London. You grew up in Bristol and went to schools in the city. At 19, after a gap year, you went to university to study Creative Music Technology. You sing in a band and play several instruments. From a young age, you always wanted to get into the music industry and, on graduation, found it really difficult to break in. Last summer, you were at Glastonbury and you got talking to a guy who works at a record label who said he was looking for a couple of new runners. You emailed him straight after Glastonbury and he called you in for a meeting and you got the job. You work really long hours but do not mind because you are meeting bands, working on pop videos and going to gigs and festivals. Recently, you met with one of the senior executives and you are in line for promotion to the new artists section, where you will be watching up-and-coming bands and advising on who looks good to sign and who does not. At home, your room is full of CDs and your iPod is jammed with all the latest albums.
- As you walk slowly, create pictures and impressions of your life so you can imagine playing in your band, the music you wrote and dreaming of working in the music industry.
- Go into real detail so you can imagine being at Glastonbury covered in mud, your ears ringing from the huge speakers and the smell of burgers forever in the air.
- Use the pictures you create to flow into the thoughts you have about yourself and other people.
- Do not force your imagination; just allow it to build slowly as you walk. If your attention goes off on to something else, slowly bring it back to your character.

Student follow-on exercise: building as you go

- The next day, at some point, bring in the pictures and impressions of your character and start to walk around the room as them. Imagine you are waiting for a band to arrive and getting a coffee. Pour the coffee, grab a biscuit and listen to the music that is playing 24/7 in your office. Then go and check your emails.
- All the time you walk around, keep imagining the pictures and impressions that you created on your walk and build on them.

Notes for the student

As you do this exercise, keep in mind Stanislavski's words: 'every one of our movements onstage, every word must be the result of a truthful imagination'.[2]

As you start to use your imagination and create pictures, you will find that your imagination gets better and better and starts to create pictures on its own. It is like making a snowman, when you start by making a ball big enough to roll and then you start to roll it and it collects snow as it goes. Your job is to start it off and keep it going in the right direction.

Notes for the teacher

I have put these two imagination exercises first so that you can send students off to start working on their imagination and then they will be able to come back and report on their progress. It means that you put the focus on them to explore and experience then return to the class to evaluate. A good grounding in using their imagination is vital for the students. I often tell students that 2 minutes imaging your characters' past and pictures of their lives here and there is far better than sitting down for an hour staring at a sheet of paper, trying to create and getting nowhere.

3 FREE BODY RELAXATION

Teacher-led exercise

AIM

To relax the body and mind.

- Imagine you are a watch engineer for Rolex. You mend and repair any watches sent to you by customers. In front of you is a vintage Rolex that has stopped. You slowly lift off the back and look for the fault.
- For 30 seconds, mend the watch, all the time imagining your surroundings and what you want to achieve.
- Keep an impression in your mind of what it was like to use your imagination.
- Now find a space on the floor and lie on your back. Place your legs about shoulder width apart and your arms by your side, with your palms facing up. Make sure your spine and neck are in a straight line and close your eyes. Your teacher or another student will now talk you through the relaxation.

Breathe in	Breathe out
Breathe in	Breathe out
Breathe in	Breathe out

Figure 1.3
Amy imagines she is fixing
a customer's watch before
the relaxation

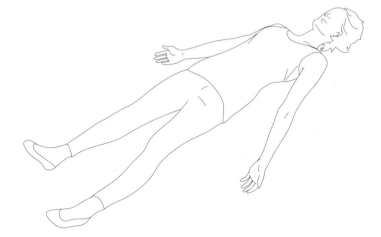

Figure 1.4
Free body relaxation

I am relaxing my toes	My toes are completely relaxed
I am relaxing my feet	My feet are completely relaxed
I am relaxing my ankles	My ankles are completely relaxed
I am relaxing my calves	My calves are completely relaxed
I am relaxing my knees	My knees are completely relaxed
I am relaxing my thighs	My thighs are completely relaxed
I am relaxing my hips	My hips are completely relaxed
I am relaxing my stomach	My stomach is completely relaxed
I am relaxing my chest	My chest is completely relaxed
I am relaxing my lower back	My lower back is completely relaxed
I am relaxing my spine	My spine is completely relaxed
I am relaxing my upper back	My upper back is completely relaxed
I am relaxing my shoulders	My shoulders are completely relaxed
I am relaxing my upper arms	My upper arms are completely relaxed
I am relaxing my elbows	My elbows are completely relaxed
I am relaxing my lower arms	My lower arms are completely relaxed
I am relaxing my hand	My hands are completely relaxed
I am relaxing my fingers	My fingers are completely relaxed
I am relaxing my neck	My neck is completely relaxed
I am relaxing my head	My head is completely relaxed
I am relaxing my face	My face is completely relaxed
I am relaxing my eyes	My eyes are completely relaxed
I am relaxing my cheeks	My cheeks are completely relaxed
I am relaxing my mouth	My mouth is completely relaxed

PAUSE

I am relaxing my mind	My mind is completely relaxed

Figure 1.5
Students relaxing

Relax for a minute or two.

Slowly, first by getting up to your knees, completely in your own time, stand up and then return to your chair.

- Now imagine you are repairing the watch again. For 30 seconds, imagine your surroundings and wanting to find out the problem with the watch, then start to repair it.

Questions for after the exercise

- Was there a difference between the first and the second time you were mending the watch?
- What was the difference?
- Did the relaxation help you to focus and use your imagination more?
- How did the relaxation make you feel?
- Do you think this is useful to you as an actor?

Notes for the student

Free body relaxation is a vital element to Stanislavski's system. As actors, we need to be in a relaxed state of mind in order to use our imaginations effectively. This exercise is designed for you to use again and again. So, before every performance or every rehearsal, you can start to get yourself into the right state of mind to work on your character. After relaxation, we find it easier to focus and hold our attention on our character. Remember, Stanislavski's system is there to help you, so lie back, relax and let your acting improve.

> **free body**
> The desired state for an actor; a body free from tension that can be used to create and experience a role.

Notes for the teacher

This exercise is a must-do exercise for early on during a unit on Stanislavski. It highlights just how important relaxation is for actors and how it can benefit them as they start to use all the different areas of the system. You can always use this exercise at the start of every lesson with a group to get them focused and ready to work. If the students have already had a busy day before they even get to you, running a free body relaxation means you will be able to get a lot more out of them in the time you have.

With the questions for after the exercise, try to identify how the watch-mending exercise was different before and after the relaxation.

4 CONCENTRATION

Student exercise

AIM

To work on your concentration and focus skills.

- Split into two groups (Group A and Group B). Group A, you are to observe to start with.
- Group B, arrange the furniture in the room in a particular way.
- Group A, watch. You have 30 seconds to memorise where everything is, then you will leave the studio.
- Group B, now rearrange the furniture in the room and then ask Group A back in.
- Group A, as you renter the room, you have to rearrange all the furniture back into the original position.
- Group B, check to see if Group A got it right.
- Group A, take ten different objects and arrange them around the room. Let Group B observe them, then ask Group B to leave the room.
- Group A, now rearrange the objects and take one away from the ten.
- Group B, come back in and rearrange the objects in exactly the right place and, as quickly as you can, say which one is missing.

Student follow-on exercise: *Bacchus and Ariadne*

- Google Titian's painting *Bacchus and Ariadne*.
- Observe the painting for 30 seconds, trying to remember as much detail as you can.
- Now ask a fellow student to ask you questions about the painting to see how much you recall.
- *Bacchus and Ariadne* is at the National Gallery in London. If possible, visit the gallery and practise this exercise. Look at the painting for a couple of seconds, then look away and describe the painting to a friend or draw the outline on paper, trying to remember as much detail about the painting as you can.

Student follow-on exercise: the room

- Walk into a room you have never been in before.
- Look around for 10 seconds, taking in as much detail as you can.
- Now go outside the room and describe it exactly to a fellow student.
- Both enter the room and see how much you remembered.

5 COMMUNICATION

Student exercise

AIM

To practise using invisible **rays**.

Stanislavski believed that we use **communication** in three ways: through movement, voice and the use of invisible rays. These rays are an invisible current that flows between us. In this exercise, we are going to locate these rays so we can then use them when acting.

- Five students stand in a line in front of the rest of the group.
- The first person in the line needs to think of a colour.
- Without using your voice or facial expression, just invisible rays, send your colour to the next person in the line.
- Turn around to face him or her, look into his or her eyes and send the colour. Imagine the colour in your mind and think of sending it to him or her.

rays
An invisible current that flows between us all the time.

communi-cation
The sending out and receiving of signals between two living beings.

Figure 1.6
Communication 1

Figure 1.7
Communication 2

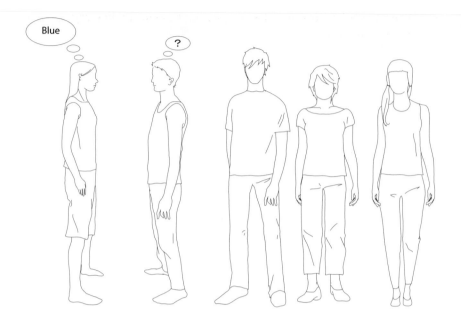

- The person receiving, just open your mind to receiving the colour. The first colour that pops into your mind is the one you then send to the next person in line.

Figure 1.8
Communication 3

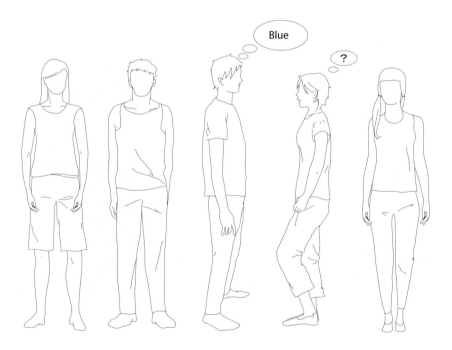

- When the colour reaches the end, go back down the line saying what colour you received.

Blue

Figure 1.9
Communication 4

- For those watching, check if you knew the colour being sent or if you could see them sending and receiving using invisible rays.

Figure 1.10
Hannah, on the right, is sending her colour to Amy. When you look into her eyes, you can see a focus and a concentration of thought. This is Hannah communicating with Amy using rays

Student follow-on exercise: human spirit of a role

Stanislavski said, 'Communication through the mind constitutes one of the most important dynamic actions in acting and should be valued. It is absolutely essential in the process of creating and emitting the life of the human spirit of a role'.[3]

- What do you think Stanislavski meant by 'the human spirit of a role'?
- Having done the communication exercise, did you start to understand the spiritual side of acting and the system?

Notes for the student

With this exercise, you not only need to be highly focused, but you need to keep an open mind to experiencing the exercise. Stanislavski believed in the combination of the mind, body and spirit when acting, and this exercise helps you to locate the more spiritual side of acting. You will need to be 100 per cent focused for this exercise to work. Much of Stanislavski's system only really works if you are completely committed and willing to explore and experiment.

Recently, I ran this workshop in a school in Surrey and the boys, from the outset, thought this exercise could not work. As actors, they did not allow themselves to give it a go, and the result was that they, as a group, never really understood this important element of the system.

The next day, I was up at a new academy in Birmingham and I did the same exercise. This time, the students were fully engaged and open to experimenting. The colour went down the line and then the students revealed the colour they had received: blue, blue, blue, blue and blue.

For some of you, this exercise may not work the first time, in which case you will need to practise it a few times. Think of it as opening the channel to communicating, but once this is open you will be able to communicate using rays and this will enable you to communicate fully on stage or on screen.

I sometimes practise with my two children over dinner. We send each other colours and see how many we get right. After a while, my seven year old and four year old begin to get adventurous and start sending Harry Potter characters!

UNDERSTANDING STANISLAVSKI THROUGH PRACTICE: WORK ON A ROLE

6 THE SIX W'S

Student exercise

AIM

To build the circumstances of your character.

•   Ask yourself the following questions, using the answers to build your character's given circumstances:

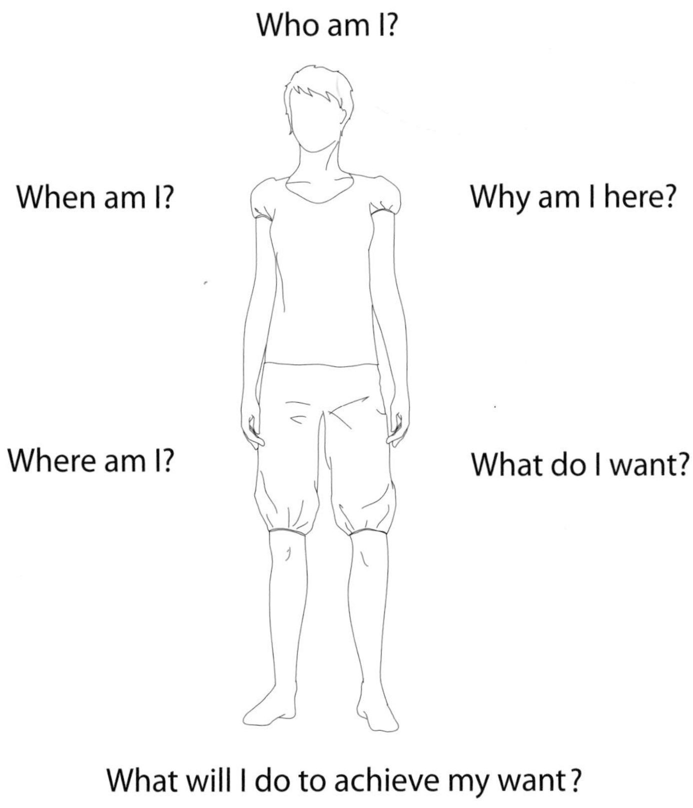

Who am I?

When am I?   Why am I here?

Where am I?   What do I want?

What will I do to achieve my want?

Figure 1.11
The six W's

Notes for the student

The first three questions will often come from the text you are working on. If you are devising, you will have to create this from the discussions you have as a group. 'Why am I here?' starts you on the road to analysing what your character is thinking and doing. The last two questions will start you thinking about your objective and action (which we will be looking at next). For you, as an actor, these questions will form the foundation for your character and are always a great way to start your analysis of your character. For those of you auditioning for drama school, or who have limited time to prepare for an audition, asking these questions and deciding on the answers will start to point you in the right direction for creating your character.

Student follow-on exercise: scene and character

- Using the last play that you read, choose a scene and a character.
- Ask yourself the six W's and see how that helps you to understand what your character is thinking and doing.

7 THE OBJECTIVE

Student exercise

AIM

To understand how to have an objective within a given circumstance.

In any given circumstance, we need to decide what we want to achieve. It is this 'want' that drives us as the character. This 'want' is our objective.

- You are going to be making a cup of tea.
- At home in your kitchen, make a cup of tea three times. As you make the tea, think about your surroundings, the weight of the cup before and after the water is poured in, the steam coming off the kettle, the room you are in and the order in which you do everything.
- Now go into a different room and imagine you are making the cup of tea, but this time without the objects and without the kitchen.
- You need to imagine the kitchen, the circumstances, your objective (what you want to achieve), what you have been doing so far today and what you will be doing later.

Figure 1.12
Millie making tea. In her
hand is the milk and she is
pouring it into the mug

- So, for my character, I imagine I have just got up and I have got to leave for college in half an hour. I have had a shower so I am going to have tea and toast before I leave. I imagine having just woken up and the kitchen around me. I imagine the steam off the kettle and the toast in the toaster. I decide what I want, my objective, and then I imagine that. Then I imagine what I am going to be doing for the rest of the day and start to prepare myself for lessons. So I would have the objective, 'I want to prepare myself for today's lessons', I would imagine going into college, sitting down thinking what we did last lesson and what we would be doing in today's lesson.

  Alternatively, my character could have got up late and only have a couple of minutes to quickly have a cup of tea before diving out the door. My objective then would be very different.

In Table 1.1, I have listed some objectives to help with this exercise.

Notes for the student

When deciding on your objective, think about the circumstances you are in and let them guide you. Although you 'want to make a cup of tea', you will need to dig a little deeper to find your real objective. This process is the start of you as the character delving into your character's **subconscious** to decide on what you really want. Often, characters want one thing on the surface and another thing underneath. It is locating what they want underneath that will help us to create believable and truthful characters.

subconscious
The part of the mind that influences our thoughts and actions without us being aware of it.

Table 1.1 Objectives

I want to do my best	I want to be the winner
I want to find out	I want to orientate
I want to suffer	I want to be superior
I want to be special	I want to belong
I want to be cared for	I want to be liked
I want to lose myself	I want to be important
I want to provoke anger	I want to be the centre of attention
I want to do my duty	I want to impress
I want to be admired	I want to be powerful
I want to be remembered	I want to be envied
I want to be rich	I want to be poor
I want to have no responsibilities	I want to be famous
I want to be strong	I want to have peace of mind
I want to enjoy my time	I want to succeed
I want to understand	I want to be rejected
I want to please	I want to despair
I want to be frustrated	I want to be accepted
I want to be lucky	I want it over and done with

When you have practised three times with the objects and three times without, go in front of your class to show them the exercise and see if they can guess what your objective was.

Stanislavski called this exercise 'action without objects', and he practised this every day for 15 to 20 minutes to keep himself stage ready. In Table 1.2 are some more actions to practise without objects.

Table 1.2 Action without objects

Shaving

Putting on make-up

Cleaning a rifle

Playing the piano

Massaging

Cooking

Washing up

Brushing your teeth

Student follow-on exercise: deciding on the objective

- Look at the scenario below and, using the list of objectives in Table 1.3, see if you can come up with an objective for both.

Table 1.3 Cat and Jen

- Cat and Jen work together in a small office. They have been working together for around 3 years and get on really well. Cat is the quieter of the two and has a very dry sense of humour; Jen is quite feisty, a good-time girl and a real 'looker'.

- Jen's boyfriend Toby, an actor, is always popping into the office when he is in town. This morning, he pops into the office when Jen is out at a meeting. Toby is chatting to Cat when his phone rings and he walks into the reception to take the call. Cat overhears the conversation and realises that Toby is seeing someone else behind Jen's back.

- Toby has to dash off and, an hour later, Jen arrives back in the office. Jen is very happy and tells Cat that she got a text from Toby saying he is meeting her after work as he has something important to tell her. Jen thinks he is going to pop the question!

- Work out, based on this scenario, what Cat's objective will be. You will first need to decide if Cat is going to tell Jen. You need to think about what Cat really thinks of Jen and how that will affect the objective you give her.
- Now imagine Cat has told Jen and decide upon Jen's objective. She could have anything from 'I want him to suffer' to 'I want to be cared for'.
- You can then improvise the scene with the objectives and see how well they work. Guys, you can do the same, but with Chris and Jake instead.

8 THE ACTION

Student exercise

AIM

To experience having an action within a circumstance.

The action is what we do to achieve our objective.

- Student A, you are a jewel thief known as Antonia. You are an expert safe cracker and have eluded the police for many years. You have a reputation for being highly professional and highly cautious.
- Student B, you are an undercover policeman, Francis. You have been tracking a jewel thief, known only as Antonia, for over 2 years and whenever you seem to get close she disappears. You have managed to arrange a meeting with a lady you think to be Antonia where you hope to lure her into stealing a tiara from a stately home so you can catch her red-handed.
- The meeting will take place at a disused car park on the outskirts of town. Antonia, you have been watching the car park for 3 hours and see the person you are to meet pull up in a car. He walks around and you slowly start to walk up to him.
- Antonia, your first action is 'I find out'. Everything you say, do and think will be with the action 'I find out'. You want to figure out if he is genuine or if he is police.
- Francis, your action is 'I do my best'.
- The improvisation starts where Antonia is seen by Francis.
- Halfway through the improvisation, Antonia, you sense something is wrong and start to walk away. Your action becomes 'I reject'. Francis, your action becomes 'I panic', quickly followed by 'I provoke interest', as you make a last ditch effort to keep Antonia talking.
- Improvise the scenario going from one action to the next action.

Questions for after the exercise

- How did having an action help your improvisation?
- Did you allow the circumstances to feed into the action?
- Did having an action help you to know what to think and do in the circumstance?

Notes for the student

psycho-physical
The combination of what we are thinking and doing that works across the system. What we think and do working together in harmony.

For those of you that have never done an action improvisation before, the best thing to do is put yourself within the circumstance, think of your action and go for it, and then evaluate what happens afterwards.

Stanislavski wanted actions to be **psychophysical** – a combination of what we are thinking and physically doing. Think about whether your actions were more psychological or more physical so that, in the follow-on exercise, you can start to redress the balance. Actions are at the heart of Stanislavski's system, and you will be using them throughout your acting career. Improvising with actions is key to the rehearsal process as you will see when we get to **active analysis** later in this chapter. Working with actions creates truthful and active theatre. All you need to do now is practise using them.

Acting tip

As actors, we do not *show* an emotion; we *have* an action within a given circumstance that creates an emotion. I do not show 'anger'; I have the action 'I tell off', which creates the emotion 'anger'.

> **active analysis**
> A rehearsal technique where actors analyse a bit of the play 'on their feet'. The actors decide on the main event, an action for each character, then improvise that bit.

Student follow-on exercise: scenario and setting

- Choose a scenario and setting from Table 1.4 and an action from Table 1.5.
- In pairs, improvise in that setting with different actions.
- Think about having a psychophysical action and, if you find an action that you cannot hold, remember that is the action you will need to practise.

Table 1.4
Scenario and setting

- *Customs*
  – being stopped and asked to empty your case.
- *Shopping centre*
  – bumping into a well-known actor.
- *Hospital*
  – meeting an old flame.
- *Building site*
  – being told you have put the wall in the wrong place.
- *Street*
  – being stopped and searched by a police officer.

Table 1.5 Actions

I enjoy	I brush off	I long for	I pity myself
I look forward	I despair	I condescend	I lose myself
I orientate	I find a reason	I get a grip on myself	I blame
I belong	I humble myself	I despair	I suffer
I provoke interest	I impress	I flirt	I provoke irritation
I take pride	I find out	I relax	I punish
I cajole	I denigrate	I bide my time	I put down
I cover up	I do my duty	I tease	I envy
I force myself	I tempt	I provoke anger	I reflect
I remember	I rehearse	I needle	I regret
I scream for help	I shrink	I search for clues	I tell off
I wait	I fascinate	I demand obedience	I plot
I tease	I divulge	I insult	I panic
I revel	I observe	I assess	I protest
I stand my ground	I dread	I pass my time	I challenge
I work myself up	I do my best	I let go	I question
I lure	I reject	I cringe	I gorge myself
I taunt	I provoke fear	I dream	I sulk
I sneer	I gloat	I entice	I brace myself
I coax	I seduce	I fascinate	I postpone

9 THE SUPER OBJECTIVE

Student exercise

super objective
The theme of the play; the sum of all the objectives of the characters; what the play is really about. For a character, the super objective is what they want over the course of the play.

AIM

To understand how to decide on a character's **super objective**.

- Choose one character from Table 1.6.

Table 1.6 Characters

Dracula	Jane Eyre
Spiderman	Mary Poppins
Sherlock Holmes	Hermione Grainger
Hamlet	Juliet
Macbeth	Lady Macbeth

- What do you think the character wants/wanted to achieve from his or her life, based on all the facts you know about him or her?
- Stanislavski said, 'We must remember the basic principle of our school of acting: the subconscious through the conscious'.[4]
- Look again at the 'want' you decided on and try to take a journey into the subconscious to decide what you think the character really wants.

Notes for the student

germ
The essence or seed of a character.

The super objective is a very useful element of the system. Combined with the **germ**, it will form the basis of your character. Together they tell you what you want and what you are like, so you know your character's future and what your character is like based on past experiences (the germ).

With the super objective, you have a direction to go in that will always keep you on the right track and, because you have delved into the subconscious of your character, you will start to unlock the all-important subtext.

You also have a super objective for a play, which we will look at in the next section.

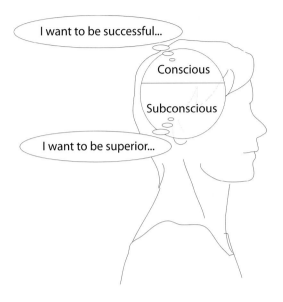

Figure 1.13
Conscious | subconscious

Acting tip

At the top of your script, write your super objective and germ, then you will always have an anchor to your character.

10 THE GERM

Student exercise

AIM

To decide on the character's germ.

The character's germ is their essence, one word that sums up their character.

- Using the character you chose from the previous exercise, now decide on your character's germ. One word, based on all your character's experiences to date, that sums up what he or she is like and what he or she thinks about himself or herself. You can use Table 1.7 to help.

- Remember to dip into the character's subconscious, thinking about the character's past experiences as a way to decide on the character's germ.

Table 1.7 Character germs

I am capable	I am innocent	I am a genius
I am lonely	I am a victim	I am cocky
I am devious	I am a winner	I am irritating
I am brave	I am selfish	I am lost
I am a cheeky little boy	I am superior	I am inferior
I am lazy	I am conscientious	I am cheeky
I am a loser	I am desirable	I am a joker
I am special	I am damaged	I am lucky
I am confused	I am a hero	I am misunderstood
I am a witch	I am frightened	I am unloved
I am a reject	I am weak	I am strong
I am devious	I am vicious	I am trapped

11 TEMPO-RHYTHM

Student exercise

AIM

To work out a character's **tempo-rhythm**.

tempo-rhythm
Our pace, both mental and physical; the pace of everything around us and everything we do.

'Where there is *life* there is *action*, and where there is *action* there is *movement*, and where there is *movement* there is *tempo*, and where there is tempo there is rhythm.'[5]

- Choose one object from the list in Table 1.8.
- Imagine your object, what it looks like, what it feels like, what sound it makes. Then, holding these things together, clap the tempo-rhythm of your object.
- The rest of the group, watch and listen, and see if you can guess the object.

Student follow-on exercise: clap the character

Stanislavski said, 'Tempo-rhythm cannot only prompt the right feelings and experiences intuitively, directly and immediately, it can help to create characters'.[6]

- With this in mind, clap out the tempo-rhythm for the five characters in Table 1.9.

Table 1.8 Tempo-rhythm

• Chair	• Oven	• Waterfall
• Telephone	• Shower	• Pond
• iPod	• Banana	• Mountain range
• Light bulb	• Glass of Coke	• Desert

Table 1.9
Five characters

- The boss of a bank who has just been told that one of her junior traders lost £10 million on a trade that had not been sanctioned.

- A recent university graduate attending his first interview.

- A computer programmer designing new software.

- A dancer in a musical.

- A librarian stacking books on a Tuesday morning.

Figure 1.14
Hannah claps out a tempo-rhythm. She has put herself in active imagination and started clapping

Notes for the student

When we are working on our character using the system, we can sometimes lose track of the character as a whole. That is when I suggest gently holding together the areas of the system that you have worked on and clapping out their tempo-rhythm, and see what happens. Think about how this helps to cement an idea of the character in your mind.

Then try placing your character in a circumstance and clapping the tempo-rhythm to see how your character reacts and responds to the circumstances. This exercise will help you reach beyond the mind and body and start to understand the spiritual.

Notes for the teacher

For you, the teacher, tempo-rhythm can be a handy tool to help students to understand their characters. When a student is struggling, I will often ask him or her to clap his or her character and then the circumstance, and then use that to move forward. It also works as a way into combining the mind, body and spirit so the students start to see the spiritual side of Stanislavski's system.

Before moving on to exploring and working on your chosen text, it is a good idea to practise using all these areas of the system that students have worked on. The following exercise is designed with that in mind. Often, students benefit from using the system practically, without text, before using the different elements with a play.

Teacher follow-on exercise: life in art

- *Choose a painting with a number of different characters in it.*
- *Show the painting to the students and tell them they are going to use all the different areas of the system that they have experienced to bring the painting to life.*
- *Cast the parts and tell the students that they are going to go away to research and then start to create their characters.*
- *They will need to use their imaginations to create the given circumstances and the pasts of their characters.*
- *They will need to work out their characters' super objectives, germs and tempo-rhythms, and decide on their objectives and actions within the circumstances.*
- *Ask your group to improvise the minute leading up to the painting and then freeze in the exact position of the painting.*
- *Remind the students to use free body relaxation and nonverbal communication during their rehearsals.*

USING STANISLAVSKI WITH TEXT

12 READING THE PLAY

Student exercise

AIM

To gain your first impression of the play.

- As a group, sit in a circle and, taking turns to read different parts, read through your chosen play.
- Think about what the play is about and what your first impressions of the play are.
- Jot down one sentence that, for you, captures the plot of the play, and then compare with the rest of your group.
- As a group, come up with one sentence that, for all of you, best sums up the plot of the play.

Student follow-on exercise: research

- Research the time that the play was written in and look at photos (if possible) and pictures of people that lived at that time.
- Come up with the ten most important **events** of the play.
- As a group, come up with a starter super objective for the play – what you think the play is really about and the direction it is going in. This is only a starter super objective and can be developed during the rehearsal process and then finalised at the *mise en scène* stage.

> **event**
> Something that happens that affects what you are thinking and doing.

13 MY CHARACTER'S PAST

Student exercise

AIM

To actively imagine your character's past.

- Imagine the life of your character from the first memory to the start of the play.
- Remember to include the major milestones in your character's life.
- Walk through major events that have happened, imagining other people and what they have said and done.
- With a partner, improvise three major events from your past, evaluating how you felt about them and the thoughts that came from them.
- Now go before your class and tell them who you are, talking through your life, as your character. Remember to start with, 'I am . . .'

14 PINNING DOWN MY CHARACTER

Student exercise

> **through action**
> What the character does to achieve his or her super objective.

> **AIM**
>
> To decide on your character's super objective, germ and **through action**.

- As your character, decide on your super objective and germ. Think about what you want to achieve in the future and the essence of your character.
- Use these as starters. Remember that, as the rehearsal process goes on, you will develop and fine tune them.
- Think about what your character subconsciously wants and is like. It is always a good idea to check with other cast members to see what they think of your decisions.
- Decide on your character's through action. Think of all the main actions you, as your character, have and then decide on one main action that you do to achieve your super objective.

Student follow-on exercise: relationships

> **relationships**
> The thoughts we have about others.

- Write down all the characters in the play that you have **relationships** with. This will include characters that you are aware of, but may never have met, and have come to some conclusions about based on what others have said.
- For each character, write down what you think of them. Try to sum up everything you feel for them in one brief statement.
- So, if I was playing Romeo, I would write down, 'Juliet is . . .'. Then every time I look at Juliet I know what to think about her.

Figure 1.15
Students discussing the super objectives of the characters they are working on

Acting tip

We do not show our relationships with others on stage. We imagine them and use invisible rays to allow them to be communicated.

15 DIVIDING UP THE PLAY

Student exercise

AIM

To divide the play into manageable **bits**.

- As a group, go through the play and divide it into 'bits'. A new bit starts when:

  - a character enters or exits;
  - there is an event on stage; or
  - there is a change of objective for one or more of the characters.

> **bit**
> A play is divided up into manage-able sections or units by the actors and director.
> A bit starts when there is an event on stage, the character's objectives change or a character enters/exits.

- Give each bit a name and a number so that it is easy to remember. If there is a fight in your play, label that bit 'fight' so, when you come to rehearse that bit, you can refer to it by name and everyone will know which bit it is.
- Do not forget to mark where each bit starts and ends on your script.

16 OBJECTIVES AND ACTIONS

Student exercise

> **AIM**
>
> To decide on an objective and action for each bit.

- Go through each bit of the play your character is in and decide on your objective and action for each bit.
- You can use the objectives in Table 1.1 and the actions in Table 1.5 from earlier in this chapter to help.
- Mark your objectives and actions in Table 1.10 and also in the margin of your script.
- On the grid in Table 1.10, you also have a box for the super objective, germ and through action so you can keep these in mind while you analyse each bit of the play.
- If you are working together as a cast, you can do this process for the first few and then you can each go home and work them out for your respective characters.

> **inner monologue**
> The thoughts going through a character's mind.

Table **1.10** Analysis grid

Super objective		Germ	Through action	
Bit name and number	Main event in the bit	Your character's objective	Your character's action	**Inner monologue**
1		I want to . . .	I . . .	I . . .
2				
3				
4				
5				
6				

Notes for the student

How you do this exercises depends on the amount of time you have. If you are working on an extract from a play, you may want to work through the majority of bits together or largely work at home and then come in and share your work. Do not worry if you are not sure of some of the objectives or actions because the next exercise, active analysis, will help to pin them down.

17 ACTIVE ANALYSIS

Student exercise

AIM

To actively analyse and stand up bits of the play.

- Read a bit of the play and decide on the main event in that bit.
- Discuss the given circumstances of the bit. You can use Exercise 6 on the six W's to help.
- Decide on an action for each character in that bit.
- Without your script, improvise the bit using the given circumstance and action to guide you.
- Evaluate the improvisation and decide if the action you had fitted the scene, and, if not, decide upon another action. It may be that, through improvising, you discover an action that works well, in which case jot that action down to use in the future.
- Read the scene again so that in the next improvisation you can start to get closer to the text.
- Decide on your objective, check your relationships with those on stage and start to bring in an impression of your super objective, germ and through action.
- Allow your improvisation to slowly start to gel all the areas of the system that you have worked on in this chapter.
- Improvise the scene again – do not think about the text; just relax and let the action, objective and the given circumstance do their work.
- Discuss the scene again and then read over the text. This process will start to see you combining the thoughts and actions of the character with the text. Each time you improvise, you will come closer to the text.

Acting tip

As actors, we do not stand on stage and try to remember lines; we put ourselves in a circumstance with an action and allow the lines to come from there.

Notes for the student

Once you have rehearsed using active analysis, you will probably be wondering why so many rehearsals are run with actors walking around a stage, script in hand, using their voice to show their character! I am still trying to figure that one out.

I have run this exercise with hundreds of groups and am yet to meet a student that does not think this improves their performance. So, from now on, leave the script down, start improvising and thinking and doing as your character. Do not worry about your lines. After using active analysis, you will find that the lines have almost stuck in your mind and become attached to the action and circumstances.

This exercise allows you to **experience** your character. You will start to move around the stage, driven by your action, and doing as your character would do.

Active analysis is very much an organic process, out of which comes the movement and voice of your character. If you have an urge to move, then move and think about and evaluate it afterwards. Remember what you did in the improvisations, but do not try to copy it the next time you rehearse that bit; just put yourself in the circumstance and 'do' your action.

experience
The state where you leave the actor behind and find the character, with everything you do being the product of your character's thoughts and actions.

Notes for the teacher

For many of you, a lot of your time will have been spent getting students to learn their lines. Active analysis means that students will have built a foundation based on improvisation, upon which they can then add the lines. Active analysis, because it is improvisation-based, will create freer and more truthful stage acting than rehearsing script in hand. It also allows the students to discover, for themselves, what to do as their characters rather than relying on being told. For most groups, it takes a few attempts, but once mastered they generally do not look back! They embrace the freedom to create, experience and explore on stage.

18 *MISE EN SCÈNE*

Teacher-led exercise

AIM

To put the finishing touches to the performance.

- *You have watched the play after the active analysis stage and now your job is to put the finishing touches to the play in line with the agreed super objective.*
- *Watch the performance and then give notes and work on key scenes where you can model the students using the super objective of the play as your guide.*
- *Remember psychophysical works both ways from the 'in out' and the 'out in'. So, if a student has trouble with his or her character, you can model his or her movements, which will then help to trigger the character's inner life.*
- *Use this time to add some impressive moments to the staging and add some comedy. Remember to tell the students to work your direction into their characters, so giving purpose and actions to your direction.*

Notes for the teacher

This is your opportunity to really add something to the play. The actors on stage cannot see the play from the outside so they will need your guidance. Be decisive in your direction so the students know what you want them to do, and do not be afraid to go back on something you asked if you realise it does not work. It is far better to say, 'that does not really work' and try something else rather than sticking to a bad idea. Remember that, for most students, if they worked through this chapter, the results will have organically come from the characters' actions, so do not start telling them what to do and where to stand unless they really need it!

You will always have a few students who are slightly lost on stage, so use actions to guide them in what to do and physically help them with their characters, and watch that start to permeate to the characters' inner lives. Do not forget about costumes and props. Once you give a student actor a uniform, a gun and camouflage cream, it is almost impossible to stop his or her imagination from creating a character!

19 THE FINAL RUN

Student exercise

AIM

To finalise, polish and set ready for the opening performance.

- Try to make sure your final run is 24 hours before the first performance to give yourself time to evaluate your performance.
- Before you go on stage, use Exercise 3 on free body relaxation and then gently start to allow your imagination to bring in your past, daily life and what you want.
- Backstage, imagine the circumstances, your objective and action, remind yourself of your relationships and then let go.
- Walk out on stage and think as the character, trusting that all the work you have done in this chapter will be there.
- Go for it and enjoy your role. When you come off stage, you can evaluate what was there and what was not ready for your first performance.
- Stanislavski wanted us to experience a role using the rehearsal technique active analysis.
- When rehearsing, we improvise with an action, within a circumstance, to organically experience what our character is thinking and doing.

SUMMARY: STANISLAVSKI AND THE SYSTEM

Imagination is your ability as the actor to treat fictional circumstances as if they were real.

When using our imagination, we create active pictures and impressions in our mind's eye.

As actors, to use our imaginations effectively, we need to be in a relaxed state of mind and body.

Stanislavski believed we communicate in three ways: through our voice, our body and using invisible rays.

The objective is what we, as the character, want to achieve within a given circumstance.

The action is what we do to achieve that objective.

The super objective is what we want over the course of our lives or the duration of the play, the germ is the essence of our character and the through action is what we do to achieve our super objective.

Tempo-rhythm is our mental and physical pace and the pace of everything around us.

It is tempo-rhythm that links the mind, body and spirit together in harmony.

2 Brecht
(1889-1956)

political
Relates to the government of public affairs and the running of the state.

social
Concerns the relationship between people and communities within a country.

From our work on the Stanislavski system, we will now move on to looking at exercises that will help us to understand how to use Bertolt Brecht's ideas on theatre and the tools that will help us start to think and work like a Brechtian actor. We will then progress on to how to use Brecht when working with text or rehearsing a play/part of a play.

The best way to approach Brecht is from the practical experience of using Stanislavski (as hopefully you are doing). Brecht's practices are best built on the foundation that Stanislavski's system gives you. Brecht believed in using a number of the exercises that you will have experienced in Chapter 1 on Stanislavski and adapting them in order to create characters that deliver a **political** and **social** message.

The majority of actors that Brecht would have used when working on his plays would have been trained using the Stanislavski system. This chapter will consist of exercises that help to shift the focus of acting to achieving Brecht's primary aim: creating a political theatre that communicates and educates its audience.[1]

Whereas Stanislavski wanted his audience to leave the theatre having lost themselves in the characters and plot, having watched people live their lives as though unobserved, Brecht wanted his audience to leave the theatre having been moved to change the social and political make-up of society, to redress the injustices and to demand a fairer, more egalitarian life. Brecht wanted:

> to develop the means of entertainment into an object of instruction, and to change certain institutions from places of amusement into organs of public communication.[1]

Brecht's work and ideas were deeply influenced by the social, political and cultural events that surrounded him, and one of your first tasks is going to be to research and understand the time in which Brecht worked. As an actor, to understand and to be able to experience Brecht, you first need to understand the environment he was working in. For Brecht, growing up in Germany, witnessing defeat in 1918, the Treaty of Versailles, the reparation years and then the rise of fascism all would greatly have affected his thoughts, ideas, and practices, and had a profound effect on the theatre he created and aspired to.

This chapter will be Brecht in practice, how you as the student and actor can explore and experience Brecht's style of theatre and acting. Like many practitioners, Brecht in theory is not always the same as Brecht in practice. By doing the exercises in this chapter, you will start to have a solid understanding of how the Brechtian actor worked and how to create and explore Brecht's theatre.

UNDERSTANDING BRECHT THROUGH PRACTICE

20 THE NARRATOR

Teacher-led exercise

> **AIM**
>
> To start to take the first steps to **narrating** and informing your audience.

narrating
The telling of a story.

- Line up in pairs at opposite sides of the room. Be as far away from each other as you can within the space you have.
- One side of the room, you are 'A', and the other side 'B'.
- 'A's, look at the 'B' opposite you. You are now partners as in Figure 2.1.
- 'A's, you need to now think of a nursery rhyme.
- 'A's, you now have to inform your partner of your nursery rhyme without at any point saying or mouthing your nursery rhyme.
- Use whatever methods you can to let the other person know what your nursery rhyme is.
- 'B's, when you know what the nursery rhyme is, put your hand up and wait for everyone else to finish.
- Now go down the line saying what you think your partner's nursery rhyme was.
- Now swap over. This time, 'B's, you have to think of a well-known song to inform your partner. When you have thought of a song, you can start to inform your partner of your choice.

Figure 2.1
Narrating

- 'B's, imagine that it is incredibly important that you get this message across, so you have to get your partner to understand what your song is.
- Remember, you cannot speak or mouth the words.
- 'A's, when you know what song it is, put your hand up.

Questions for after the exercise

- How did you communicate your nursery rhyme or song to your partner?
- When you could not use your voice to communicate, what did you use instead?
- Did you feel that you started to use your body and physicality to directly communicate with your partner?

Notes for the student

In this exercise, you will find that you start to narrate your message – here, the nursery rhyme or song – through physical movements and expressions to your partner. As we develop using Brechtian techniques, this message will become a political and social one that you then need to communicate to your audience. There is a temptation when starting to use Brechtian technique to throw away all that you have learnt through your work on the

Stanislavski system and just 'show' and fully externalise your character. Instead, try to think of it as shifting the focus of the skills you have learnt working on Stanislavski's system to communicate now with a new purpose.

21 TURBULENT TIMES

Student exercise

> **AIM**
>
> To understand the political, social and cultural backdrop to Brecht's work.

- Start to find out as much about the time that Brecht worked in that you can.
- Draw up a timeline of the major events that occurred during Brecht's lifetime.
- Research the following subjects in Table 2.1.
- Print out a map of Europe today and a map of Europe in 1914, 1920, 1939 and 1950, and think about how the geographical differences in the make-up of Europe may have affected Brecht and his work.

Table 2.1
Research

Communism
Marx
Egalitarian society
Fascism
The rise of Hitler

Student follow-on exercise: Brecht the playwright

- Choose two of Brecht's plays from Table 2.2 and read and compare them.
- What do you think is the underlying message of the two plays?
- Is the message similar in both plays that you read?

Notes for the student

Having done this exercise, you should have a good idea of the time that Brecht was working in and a knowledge of the style of plays he wrote. I recently ran a Brecht workshop in a school in Surrey and started with the first few exercises in this chapter. I soon realised that the group were not sure about the time that Brecht was working in and it meant they were not able to put Brecht's work in perspective. It helps us to imagine what life would have been like for Brecht, to help us understand where his ideas and practices came from.

A number of exercises in the rest of this chapter will be using Brecht's *The Caucasian Chalk Circle*, so reading the play before you move on to the later exercises will really help.

Table 2.2
Brecht's plays

- *The Caucasian Chalk Circle*
- *Fear and Misery of the Third Reich*
- *Mother Courage and her Children*
- *The Good Person of Szechwan*
- *The Resistible Rise of Arturo Ui*

22 CLASS

Teacher-led exercise

> **class**
> The position a person holds in society based on his or her wealth, education and upbringing.

AIM

To examine the importance of political, social and **class** issues within society today.

- Form two straight lines as quickly as you can. Face inwards so that both lines are looking at each other.
- On a word from your teacher, reorder yourselves with the tallest at one end and the shortest at the other.

Figure 2.2
Class

- Now organise yourselves in order of date of birth, with the oldest at one end and the youngest at the other.
- Next, organise yourselves in order of the number of A*'s at GCSE.

At this point, think about how you felt when you had to put yourselves in order of A*'s.

- Now form one long line. In one part of the studio, there is an abstaining area. If you wish not to take part in the next part of the activity, you can go and wait in that area. However, you will have to explain why you abstained afterwards!
- Using the left hand side of the line as **left wing** and the right hand side of the line as **right wing**, put yourselves in order of political persuasion.
- Now organise yourselves along the line, with the left being those of you who strongly agree with tuition fees and the right those who strongly disagree.
- In your straight line, organise yourselves into the number of times you have been dumped by your boyfriend/girlfriend, with the left side being the least times and the right being the most.
- Now put yourselves along the line in class order, so working class goes to the left and upper class to the right of the line.

left wing
To follow socialist views.

right wing
To follow conservative views.

Figure 2.3
Political persuasion

Left Wing

Right Wing

Notes for the student

Hopefully, this exercise has helped you to see the importance of social and political issues in society. You probably found some parts of this exercise embarrassing or difficult to do. I did this exercise in a girls' independent school and nearly all of the girls found it difficult to put themselves in a higher class above another student. Some of the girls were adamant they were working class, regardless of their upbringing and parental income. Today, we are often told that we live in a classless society, but whenever I do this exercise I find that not necessarily to be the case. You now need to start to use the feelings that have been roused in you through this exercise in order to help to communicate your chosen political and social message when acting. When, later in this chapter, we move on to looking at *The Caucasian Chalk Circle*, you will find many of the political, social and gender issues in the play are as relevant to us today as when Brecht wrote. Today, they are just a bit more hidden away.

Notes for the teacher

I usually do this exercise early on when looking at Brecht to get the students to think about class and political issues. This exercise helps to shift the focus away from thinking about the feelings of a character to the issues that exist in society. Students will often feel uncomfortable when putting themselves in class order or sharing their political beliefs, and questioning them about this will help them start to work towards creating political theatre.

23 THE TAXI DRIVER

Student exercise: paired improvisation

AIM

To use improvisation to help start to create Brechtian characters.

- Student A, you are a taxi driver parked at Kings Cross station. It is 3 o'clock in the afternoon and you have been on shift since 10 o'clock this morning.
- Student B, you will come out of the station and hail the cab. You want to go to Heathrow airport. From the list in Table 2.3, choose one of the characters and, through gestures, action, voice, body language and small talk, let the taxi driver know your class, social background, gender, ethnicity, profession and family background.

Figure 2.4
The taxi driver

- Start by signalling to the taxi driver that you want to hire the cab and then enter the taxi, remembering that everything you do, think and say sends a message to the audience about your character.
- Remember, depending on the character that you choose, you need to inform the driver and the audience about your character through your use of actions, gestures, physicality, etc.
- Use props, an umbrella, a suitcase, a hat, a newspaper to help to inform the driver of your character.
- Student A, your task is to try to figure out who they are, where they are going, how old they are, what class they come from and what job they do. Do not ask these questions straight out, but try to work it out

Figure 2.5
Michaela is playing the taxi driver with Millie playing the single mother. Within the scene, both characters started to belong with each other, with Millie choosing to sit in the front, next to the taxi driver

from student B's characterisation. When you think you know, put your hand up, shout stop and tell the audience and your passenger who you think they are.

- Once you have done one character, try others from the list and then swap around so you both get to play the taxi driver and the passenger. Think about your character as the taxi driver and the different relationships you had with each passenger.

Table 2.3 Taxi driver characters

- A plasterer, 24, from Essex running late for a flight to Malaga for a boys' holiday with six old school friends.
- A top heart surgeon, 59, on his way to an international conference of heart specialists in Berlin where he will be the keynote speaker on some groundbreaking research he has recently completed.
- A single mother, 19, on benefits with her 2-year-old daughter, going to visit her sick mother in Scotland.
- An Italian housewife, 48, visiting the grave of her mother in France. She has two children, both at university, and a husband who works in a merchant bank in the city.
- A supply teacher, 29, travelling to Sydney, Australia in search of more money and a better job.

Notes for the student

The key to this exercise is knowing what you want the audience to think about your character and then allowing yourself, through your body, facial expressions, props, and voice, to communicate this to the audience. You, as the actor, need to think about the message that your character is communicating.

For example, if you are playing the single mother on benefits, you may want to think about how to inform the audience of the imbalances and inequalities that exist in society today.

Recently, I ran a Brecht workshop with an AS group. The single mother had two bags and her toddler and was trying desperately to get into the taxi with the least amount of fuss to the driver. The same actor, when playing the heart surgeon, just stood on the side of the road gesturing with his umbrella and waited for the taxi driver to come out and get his bag. The taxi driver got out of the cab and put the case in the boot while the heart surgeon tapped him on the shoulder with his umbrella, saying, 'Good chap'. This led to a discussion about class and what the actor playing the heart surgeon was communicating to the audience.

Notes for the teacher

This exercise will help students to start to create a character to inform their audience with a message and a purpose. There is always a temptation for students, when using Brecht, to simply show at a very superficial level a character to the audience and think that is 'Brechtian'. By introducing the idea of informing the audience of the social/political message of the character, students start to see the purpose behind Brechtian theatre.

I would get students up in pairs, put out four chairs to represent the taxi and then start the improvisations, swapping over the taxi driver and passenger as you go. It is always a good idea to stop after each one and discuss what the students thought the message was and how it was communicated. I usually start to introduce **gestic props** *and gestus at this stage, and tell the students we will be moving on to that in the next couple of exercises.*

> **gestic props**
> Props that are used by the actor or director to send a message to the audience.

24 FOLDING LINEN

Student exercise

> **AIM**
>
> To practise the **externalisation** of emotion and move towards the using of **gestus**.

> **externalisation**
> To show thoughts or feelings on the outside using gesture, movement and facial expression.
>
> **gestus**
> A gesture that defines the position your character is in within society.

- Student A and student B, you are two housewives who live next door to each other. Today is wash day and you are folding up bed sheets after taking them off the washing line.
- Your husbands are sitting in the garden next to you, which is behind a low wall. They are smoking and relaxing.
- You both start to have an argument purely for the benefit of your husbands. Use your voices and physicality to let your husbands know that you are having an argument.
- Then do the exercise again but in silence, thinking about how you can externalise the argument through facial expressions and physicality.
- Try to find one movement or gesture that sums up what you want the audience to understand about how you feel.

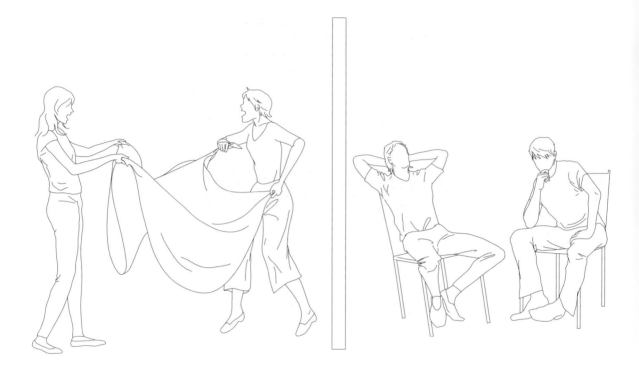

Figure 2.6
Folding linen

Student follow-on exercise: tempers flare

- Start the argument again, but this time the argument becomes real. One of you can make a comment about the other's husband that is too personal or let slip something you should not have.
- Improvise the exercise going into the full-blown argument.

Questions for after the exercise

- How did you feel folding the sheets while, at the same time, pretending to be having an argument?
- Did you find you started to externalise your emotions?
- Did you find you were coming up with a particular physical movement that helped to express your character?
- Was there any message behind the improvisations? Were you telling the audience anything about your class or social status?

Notes for the student

Brecht used this exercise to help his actors externalise their emotions and separate what they were doing physically from what they were saying. He wanted his actors to break up their own speech patterns and start to narrate when they acted. Then, when he moved them on to working on a text, the actors would be thinking about how they could represent their characters within their historical situation and inform the audience about the society they lived in. This exercise is the first step to acting with gestus. Gestus is the replacement of the psychophysical action that we used in Chapter 1 on Stanislavski, with a gesture that physicalises the character's situation within the society they live. Do not worry – Exercise 27 will help you to understand how to use gestus!

25 CHARACTERISATION OF A FELLOW ACTOR

Student exercise

AIM

To practise observing how others behave and to practise working on imitation.

- Sit in a semi-circle.
- One of you goes up into the space and, using your voice, physicality, facial expressions, tempo and props, imitate one of the others in your group.
- Think about how the student you have chosen to imitate walks, how they talk, and any mannerisms they have. Think about what, through your imitation, you would like the audience to think about the person you have chosen.
- For the rest of the group, do not shout out when you know who they are imitating, but wait until they have finished and then go down the line saying who you think they were characterising.
- Then the next person goes up so you all have a go of imitating someone else in the group.

Student follow-on exercise: meeting

- In pairs, have a conversation about one of the areas taken from Table 2.4. From the start, you will be imitating your partner and your partner will be imitating you while improvising.
- Think about how you can use the audience during the improvisation to help them know what kind of person your partner is.
- Think about comedy and how effectively this can be used to get your message across about what the other person is like.

Table 2.4 Meeting scenarios

1 Results day and you have both just received your results.
2 Talking about a new boy/girl who has joined your group.
3 Reflecting on a play you both saw last week.
4 Talking about an incredibly inappropriate photo that a mutual friend has just uploaded to Facebook.
5 Arguing about whether to go to a festival in the summer, a week in Newquay or both.

Notes for the student

When you are doing this exercise, think about how you would like to present your friend and how can you let the audience know their class, social views, type of character, pet hates, physical mannerisms, accent, etc. Comedy can be a very effective tool in communicating a message to the audience. Brecht's rehearsal studio was a place of fun, as this exercise proves. Often it is the funny things that stick in our mind, which is worth remembering when you move on to creating Brechtian theatre. Brecht's style and theatre is sometimes presented as heavy and dour with overly tragic undertones when, in reality, like all theatre, an injection of comedy can work wonders.

After this exercise, think about how you presented your characterisation of your fellow actor and how you can transfer these skills when you work on a character in a play. Remember, these exercises are for you to explore and experience, try things out and make mistakes as you journey towards having a balanced understanding of how to create Brechtian theatre.

26 V-EFFECT

Student exercise

AIM

To explore how to distance the audience from empathising with the character's journey within the play.

• Read the speech from Grusha in *The Caucasian Chalk Circle*.
• Think about how you can detach yourself as the actor from the character, and start to reflect the significance of the events of the play and not just what is happening to Michael and Grusha.

- Using your voice, movement, facial expression, physicality, props, costume, sound and music, improvise the speech.
- Try to say the lines as if you are describing an accident you have observed rather than something that directly happened to you.

In this scene, Azdak the judge is asking Grusha why she thinks Michael should be given to her to look after and not his mother.

Grusha   I've brought him up 'according to my best knowledge and conscience'. I always found him something to eat. Most of the time he had a roof over his head. And I went to all sorts of trouble for him. I had expenses, too. I didn't think of my own comfort. I brought up the child to be friendly with everyone. And from the beginning I taught him to work as well as he could. But he's still very small.[2]

Notes for the student

As you do this exercise, think how you make the audience think not about how Grusha is feeling, but how society has created this situation that Grusha finds herself in. Brecht called this distancing the **v-effect**, where the actor attempts to detach himself or herself from becoming lost in the circumstances of the play while allowing himself or herself to narrate proceedings.

Brecht used the v-effect when directing a play to make the audience view the play differently to how they normally would. Brecht would use lighting, song, sound, music, narration and direct address to help the audience shift their focus and create an **epic theatre**.

Distancing or the v-effect can be quite subtle and understated in performance. As Brecht says, the aim of the v-effect 'was to make the spectator adopt an attitude of inquiry and criticism in his approach'.[3]

Student follow-on exercise 1: historicisation

- Take this short scene and improvise, including the role of the judge. Think about the different time periods in which you could set the play.
- Improvise the scene a number of times each in different time periods and see how that helps to create a v-effect.
  Brecht called this **historicisation**, where, to help distance the audience from the given circumstances of the play, he set the events of the play in the past. If Brecht wanted to highlight something wrong in today's society, he would pick a different period in which to set his play in order to show how society may or may not have changed.

v-effect
Where the actor attempts to detach himself or herself from becoming lost in the circumstances of the play, while allowing himself or herself to narrate proceedings.

epic theatre
The term used to describe theatre that uses Brecht's methods and techniques to create theatre with a political, social and economic message.

historicisation
Setting the events of a play in a different time period to help distance the audience from the given circumstances.

Student follow-on exercise 2: contrasting practitioners

- Take this short scene and now use the Stanislavski system to rehearse it and see what the differences are in the outcome.
- Think about how Stanislavski and Brecht are similar and how they can be different.

27 GESTUS

Student exercise

> **AIM**
>
> To explore the use of gestus.

- In groups of three, look at the section from *The Caucasian Chalk Circle* involving Grusha, the Elder Lady and the Younger Lady.

  The Elder Lady (imperious)   You seem to be rather clever at making beds, my dear. Let's have a look at your hands!
  Grusha (frightened)   What?
  Grusha shows the ladies her hands.
  The Younger Lady (triumphant)   Cracked! A servant!*
  The Elder Lady goes to the door and shouts for service*
  The Younger Lady   You're caught! You swindler! Just confess what mischief you're up to!
  Grusha (confused)   I'm not up to any mischief. I just thought you might take us a little way in your carriage.* Please, I ask you, don't make any noise, I'll go on my own.
  The Younger Lady (while the elder lady continues shouting for service)   Yes, you'll go all right, but with the police. For the moment you'll stay. Don't you dare move, you!⁴

- In groups of three, improvise the scene.
- For each character where you see the asterisk (*), think of a gestus – a physical gesture that expresses your attitude to what is happening around you and in society.
- As you decide on this gestus, think about what you would like the audience to think about the situation. What do you want them to leave the theatre thinking?
- Work on creating and crafting a gestus that highlights how your character has been affected by the political, social and **economic** climate around you.

economic
Anything that relates to buying and selling, production and manufacturing of goods and how wealth is achieved.

Figure 2.7
Michaela and Hannah
practising gestus

Notes for the student

Whereas with Stanislavski we think about the character's inner life, with Brecht we think about our character's gestus. When you are working with gestus, you can think of it as replacing the action that you used in Chapter 1 on Stanislavski with a gesture that defines the position your character is in within society. So, in this scene, your gestus shows the moment that Grusha is rejected because of her class. The younger and elder ladies think nothing of the fate of the child but are driven by perceptions of their place in society. Through gestus, you need to relate this to the audience. You can start to think about how, as an actor and a director, you might make this short scene Brechtian by using other exercises such as the v-effect and adopting a more narrative style.

Student follow-on exercise: working on script

- Move from improvising this scene to using the text.
- Rehearse and then show the scene with your gestus at the moment highlighted.
- Start to think about characterisation and how you will communicate this to the audience.
- Work on your character's physicality and how this expresses your position within society.
- Think about costume and how this could support your character's gestus.

Notes for the teacher

I let the students explore different ways of using gestus here and allow them to think how they can create a gestus that reflects a message. Often, students will try different things before they arrive at a particular gestus. Remind students that the gestus can be quite subtle or it can be stylised where a particular moment is marked. With some groups, it helps to run the scene within the given circumstance, with each actor having an action and then running the scene again with gestus.

USING BRECHT WITH A TEXT

This next section will be using *The Caucasian Chalk Circle*, but you can use these exercises with whichever text you are currently working on. Whenever I am running a workshop on Brecht and using Brecht with a text, I always keep Peter Thomson's words on Brecht in mind:

> [Brecht's] departure from Stanislavskian methods was not total, but graduated. In the first stage of rehearsal actors should become acquainted with their characters, the second stage is one of empathy, 'and then there is a third phase in which you try to see the character from the outside, from the standpoint of society'.[5]

28 THE ENSEMBLE READ THROUGH

Student exercise

AIM

To gain an understanding of the central themes of the play.

- As a group, sit in a circle.
- Choose one person to read all the stage directions in the play.
- Start to read the play, with each person reading about two pages of text before the next person takes over.
- Do not have a part each, but just read all of the parts in your two pages.
- Do not attempt any characterisation or start to use your voice to show the character, but just read as if you were reading a story.

Notes for the student

Think of this exercise not as a read through of the play, but a chance to find out about what happens, who the characters are and how you feel about what has happened in the play. It is interesting that neither Stanislavski nor Brecht encouraged a read through where actors start to characterise their parts. As this is such a widespread practice, I often wonder how it has evolved!

Notes for the teacher

This is a good opportunity for the group right at the start of the rehearsal process to see how Brecht approached a text. It is probably a good idea to divide this up over a couple of lessons. The idea is that the students start to use the read through to think about what the play means to them and how they feel about it. Ask them to read as they would read a story rather than a play reading.

29 FIRST REACTIONS

Student exercise

> **AIM**
>
> To explore the first reactions to the play.

- After reading the play, go home and think about your first reactions to the play:

  - What did you think it was about?
  - What did you not like?
  - What surprised you?
  - What confused you?

- Then go in front of your group and tell them what you thought, answering the above points. Remember, it is not about getting it right or wrong, but relying on your instinct. Start with, 'I thought the play was about . . .', then move on to, 'I did not like . . .'.

Figure 2.8
Amy shares her thoughts on
the play with the group

Notes for the student

Brecht wanted the cast of the play not to think about the character they
would be playing, but what was surprising about the play. He wanted to
keep this element of surprise within the play so that it would be
communicated to the audience. He would want his audience to be shocked
at the events of the play, and a good way of doing that was keeping his
actors from becoming too familiar with play.

30 THE SET

Student exercise

AIM

To decide on the basic idea for the set.

- As a group, decide on your basic vision for the set.
- Think about where you will set each scene.
- Start to sketch out the main settings that will be in the play.
- Start to think about how these sets will affect the episodes of the play
  and how they can represent the attitudes of the characters on stage.

31 CASTING THE PLAY

Student exercise

AIM

To decide on casting for the play.

- When casting, think about how you can **de-familiarise** the audience through casting.
- Use cross-generational, cross-gender and cross-class casting.
- Double up parts so that the audience will not identify one character with one role.
- Start to decide how you, as a cast, can show the changes in character as they happen.
- Will you use costume, lighting or sound effects?

> **de-familiarise**
> A technique designed to make the audience stop and think about the social effects of the events on stage.

Notes for the student

Be adventurous, but at the same time do not go overboard. Having a largely male cast all running around the stage in drag, however much fun it may be, will not necessarily achieve the kind of v-effect Brecht had in mind. Think about how you can use different elements of cross-casting to cement your message in the mind of the audience.

32 EPISODES

Student exercise

AIM

To start to rehearse the play episodically.

- Mark out the major episodes in the play. Most Brecht plays follow an episodic structure; if your play does not, you can do that now.
- When you rehearse each episode, work on them out of sequence, with each one as a standalone episode.

- As you go through the rehearsal process, do not think about creating a through line of events, but think about each episode as a separate entity with its own message for the audience.

Notes for the student

Brecht's plays are largely written as episodes. When he rehearsed, he often worked on episodes out of sequence to help the actors avoid over-familiarising themselves with the play. As you work through your play, follow Brecht's lead and see what effect this has on you as an actor.

33 THE MESSAGE OF THE PLAY

Student exercise

AIM

To start to decide on the message of the play.

- As a group, think about what the central message is for the play and what you want the audience to think about as they leave the theatre.
- Think about what you want the audience to think about society, the political situation, the economic climate and the role of class.
- As a group, create a gestus for the play that will help to sum up what you want the message of the play to be.

Student follow-on exercise: a character's gestus

- At different points during your day, think about an individual character in a particular scene and decide on a gestus for that character.
- Do this exercise as you are walking home or on a break. Only spend 30 seconds to 1 minute on this and then carry on with whatever you were doing.
- Allow yourself to start to build an idea of the different characters, and a gestus for each one that best reflects their characters.
- Show these ideas to your fellow cast and discuss the effect these would have on the overall message of the play.

Notes for the student

Recently, I was working with an AS group in a school in Hadley Wood using Brecht with the Lisa McGee play *Girls and Dolls*. Two thirds of the way through the workshop, we discussed a gestus for the play and came up with the idea of a silent scream to represent the abuse that children can suffer in society. This silent scream then became part of the fabric of the play, and helped us to highlight the key message of the play and create some really interesting staging.

34 EPIZATION

Student exercise

> ## AIM
>
> To think how and for what purpose lines should be said.

*   Read the scene between Simon and Grusha in Scene 2 of *The Caucasian Chalk Circle*.

    The soldier   What! The young lady is not in church? Shirking service?

    Grusha   I was already dressed to go. But they wanted one more goose for the Easter banquet. And they asked me to fetch it. I know something about geese.

    The soldier   A goose? (*feigning suspicion*) I'd like to see that goose.

    Grusha doesn't understand.

    One has to be on one's guard with women. They say: 'I only went to fetch a goose' and then it turns out to be something quite different.

    Grusha (walks resolutely towards him and shows him the goose)   There it is. And if it isn't a fifteen pound goose, and they haven't stuffed it with corn, I'll eat the feathers.

    The soldier   A queen of a goose. It will be eaten by the Governor himself. So the young lady has been down to the river again?

    Grusha   Yes, at the poultry farm.

    The soldier   I see! At the poultry farm, down by the river. Not higher up, near those – those willows?

    Grusha   I only go to the willows to wash linen.

    The soldier (insinuatingly)   Exactly.

    Grusha   Exactly what?

    The soldier (winking)   Exactly that.[6]

- In pairs, read the scene aloud, adding 'he said'/'she said' before you say your line. So, the first two lines are said as:

  > He said, 'What! The young lady is not in church? Shirking service?'

  > She said, 'I was already dressed to go. But they wanted one more goose for the Easter banquet. And they asked me to fetch it. I know something about geese.'

- Think about what effect saying 'he said' or 'she said' has on your performance. How does it make you say the lines?
- Now decide on a more specific verb that will help you to describe how your character is saying the line. I have listed some examples to help:

she asserted	he cried
she claimed	he muttered
she whispered	he disclosed
she hinted	he joked
she screamed	he mocked
she divulged	he hinted
she complained	he snarled
she flirted	he scolded
she rebuked	he teased
she rejected	he discarded

- Write down in pencil each verb next to the line to help you when you come to read with the verbs.
- When you are choosing the more specific verb, think about how your choice of verb will end up affecting the audience. Think about what you want to tell the audience through your choice of verb when doing the **epization** exercise.
- Read the scene again with your specific verbs.

epization
A rehearsal technique used to create a narrative style of delivery of text.

Student follow-on exercise: add the adverb

- In pairs, add an adverb to your specific verb to further inform the audience about your character, the situation and the society you live in.
- Now run the scene with just the lines and see if this exercise has changed the way you rehearse the scene.
- Think about the effect that this process has on your acting.
- How does this exercise make you feel as an actor? What does it make you start to think about?

Notes for the student

This exercise is not about how well you can think up verbs so do not worry if you use the same verb a couple of times. Think of what verb would best communicate what you want the audience to understand and give it a go.

This exercise helps you to think of communicating and narrating as your character and gently moves you from working as the Stanislavskian actor to the Brechtian actor. While doing this exercise, start to think about your gestus, the play's gestus and the v-effect, and how these work together when using the epization exercise with text.

Notes for the teacher

This exercise works really well in making the student think as the Brechtian actor. After a few goes of using 'he said'/'she said', the students start to think about how they should be saying the line and that is when you can move them on to using more specific verbs. I give them a certain amount of time to work out the verbs and then let them explore away. Students then start to use the specific verb to determine how they say the line. At this point, you can ask them why they chose the verb in order to trigger off a deeper discussion on the purpose of the scene. At the end of this exercise, let them play the scene just as it is written and see how they get on and how much of an impact the epization exercise has made.

35 FEEDING LINES

Student exercise

> **AIM**
>
> To start to rehearse a scene without holding your script.

- Using the scene between Grusha and Simon from Exercise 34 on epization, have two actors feeding the lines and two actors on stage playing Simon and Grusha.
- As you move around the stage, start to think about what your position on stage tells the audience and how your movements send a message.

Notes for the student

Brecht, similar to Stanislavski, never wanted his actors to walk the stage script in hand, preferring his actors to be fed lines from the sides of the stage while they rehearsed. This further de-familiarises you, as the actor, from the through line of the play and starts you thinking of how you can communicate your gestus to the audience and highlight the social, political and economic themes of the play.

36 FREEZE AND GESTUS

Student exercise

> **AIM**
>
> To work on an individual scene in depth and develop character.

- Choose a scene from the play you are currently working on. You will be using this scene for the next few exercises.
- In a group, each take the part of one of the main characters.
- In turn, through a series of freezes, using gestus and narration, tell the story of that scene from one of the character's perspectives.
- Follow this process for all of the main characters in the scene so you will finish up having told all of the different characters' journeys.
- Think about how you can have one character narrating to the audience and use the space to create a v-effect.

Student follow-on exercise: evaluation

- Think about how each character's story was different. What does it tell you about the different characters?
- Now run the scene experimenting with how you can integrate the different characters' perspectives into the scene as a whole.

Notes for the student

Brecht's rehearsal room was a place of experimentation and fun. Brecht wanted his actors to explore experience and play with different gestus during rehearsal. I would follow Brecht's lead and use this exercise to really try things out and evaluate them afterwards to see what worked and what did not.

Figure 2.9
The girls experimenting with gestus in a scene

37 STYLISING

Student exercise

AIM

To experiment with the presentation of a scene.

- Using your chosen scene, in groups, using voice, movement, space and levels, think how you can start to stylise the scene.
- Keep in mind the message of the play you have decided upon and all the work you have done up to this point.
- Experiment with using **choral work** and working as an **ensemble** within the scene.
- Think about how you can physicalise the scene to create a v-effect and get the audience to focus on what the real message of the play is.
- Work with props to start to use them as gestus. Think back to how you used props in the taxi driver exercise at the start of the chapter.

choral work
A piece of theatre rehearsed together with the actors performing in time and to the same rhythm.

ensemble
A group of actors performing together.

Figure 2.10
Amy discussing how to stylise a scene

38 BANNERS

Student exercise

AIM

To explore the use of banners and placards.

- Using the chosen scene, create a series of banners that can be used during the scene to enhance the v-effect and to identify key messages that you want the audience to be made aware of.
- Make your banners and then rehearse using them within the scene. Be creative with your banners and try different ways of using them.
- Try using them with freezes or when a character stops mid-speech and shows the banner to the audience.
- Think about how you can use comedy with your banner to highlight your message.

39 LIGHTING

Student exercise

AIM

To explore using lighting with your chosen scene.

- With your chosen scene, work out a lighting plan.
- Decide how you would light the stage and when the lighting would change.
- When deciding on the lighting, think how you can use lighting to tell your story and deliver your group's message to the audience.
- Experiment with different lighting states and, as a group, discuss what the lighting represents and how it will affect what the audience is thinking.
- If you have not got access to lighting equipment, do not worry; you can plot each lighting state on paper and then walk around in the space describing how the lighting would be.

40 SOUND, SONG AND MUSIC

Student exercise

AIM

To explore the use of sound, song and music.

- Now add any sounds, music or song to your rehearsed scene.
- Use a range of different musical instruments to create a soundscape to your scene. A number of simple instruments is fine – a tambourine, a small flute, maracas, coconut shells. If you do not have any of these, two blocks of wood or a simple drum will work well.
- Think about how you can use these instruments within the scene.
- Add song and music to your scene, always thinking about what effect you want to create through using song and music.

Figure 2.11
Michaela, Millie and Hannah experimenting with space, levels and instruments to create a piece of epic theatre

Student follow-on exercise: choosing music

- Choose a variety of pieces of music that you think will work with this scene.
- Try out the music with your group to see which ones work best.

41 VOICING THE PART

Student exercise

AIM

To further explore distancing techniques.

- Choose a scene in the play you are working on that has two characters on stage. You can always choose the scene on page 67 between Grusha and Simon.
- Run the scene with two actors playing the characters on stage and two standing on stage in a different position (Figure 2.12).
- Rehearse the scene once with the two other actors, A and B, listening to what is said by the actors playing Simon and Grusha.

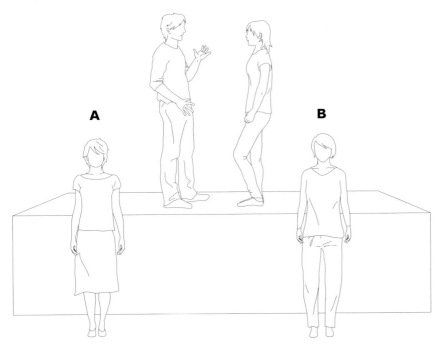

Figure 2.12
Voicing the part

- Run the scene again, with A and B voicing the lines of Simon and Grusha.
- Experiment with where A and B will position themselves and work on the scene until the timing of the voicing is right.

Questions for after the exercise

- How did you feel as actors rehearsing the scene with someone else voicing your part?
- How did you feel as the actor playing the voice?
- What effect do you think this exercise would have on the audience if used with the play?
- Did positioning A and B in different places change the scene?
- What is the effect if they voice the part off stage?

Notes for the student

Play around with where you can position the actors, A and B. Think about how you can make the scene comical or how you can make the scene more tragic. It is often by exploring ideas practically that you will come up with something that really works well and is effective. Remember, there is no right or wrong in an exercise like this; it is about you as actors finding a staging that is effective within the context of the play you are doing. The idea behind this exercise is to give you ideas that you can explore and then extend. Be creative with your ideas to see what you can produce and always have in mind what you want to achieve.

Student follow-on exercise: the Brechtian director

- Step back from the scene and play it over in your mind. Think: If I was a Brechtian director, what would I want to achieve from a scene like this?
- How does this scene help to get across the social, political and economic message?
- Try putting yourself in the director's position during rehearsal so you can view the play as the actor and the director.

42 EPIC THEATRE

Student exercise

AIM

To rehearse a piece of text using the skills learnt in this chapter.

- Using all the exercises and techniques you have explored in this chapter, you are now going to create, in your group, a piece of epic theatre.
- You can use an extract from the play you are working on or you can use the governor's wife extract from *The Caucasian Chalk Circle*. The extract is about halfway through Scene 2, where the adjutant has asked the governor's wife to get away from the town as she is in danger, while the governor's wife starts to sort out which clothes she can leave behind.
- Bring together all the previous exercises. You can use the epization exercise on the text and work through the scene using freeze and gestus.
- Experiment with the staging of the scene, paying attention to stylising the drama, using lighting, sound, music and banners.
- Be creative with the scene, creating characters that reflect the message of the scene and the piece as a whole.
- As a group, make sure you know the message you want the audience to understand and take it in turns to step into the director's shoes to ensure this message is being communicated.
- Think about everyone being on stage all the time, multi-rolling and cross-casting.
- Have your instruments on stage and ready to use.
- Think about how every movement tells part of the story to the audience.

Questions for after the exercise

- What do you thinking Brecht is telling us about class in this extract?
- What do you think the governor's wife's priority is – her material possessions or her own child?
- What do you think the social message of this extract is?

Notes for the student

While rehearsing this exercise, keep Brecht's words in the back of your mind:

> Theatre consists in this: in making live representations of reported or invented happenings between human beings and doing so with a view to entertainment.[7]

Think about how you can portray the character of the governor's wife, and how the choice you make will determine what the audience thinks of her and the society she represents.

SUMMARY: BRECHT

Brecht wanted to create an epic style of theatre that communicated a social, political and economic message to the audience.

The v-effect is where the actor and director attempt to distance the audience from losing themselves within the context of the play, instead allowing the actors to narrate proceedings and communicate the message of the play to the audience.

Brecht used historicization to help distance the audience from the given circumstances of the play by setting the events of the play in the past.

Gestus is a physical gesture that expresses the actor's and director's attitude to what is happening around them and in society.

Brecht used cross-casting, doubling and multi-role playing when rehearsing a play.

Brecht used epization exercises to enable actors to start communicating and narrating as their characters, supporting the agreed message of the play.

Stylising a scene, the use of banners, lighting, sound, song and music all play an integral part in staging a play.

Brecht's rehearsal process was one of exploration and experimentation and, ultimately, fun.

3 Lecoq
(1921–1999)

'*Toute bouche*', or 'Everything moves',[1] said Jacques Lecoq in 1997, and this remained central to his teaching. Lecoq came to theatre through sports, studied at a college of physical education, became interested in the movement of the body through space and experimented with performance that combined movement and theatre. He founded his own school in Paris in 1956, and the Ecole Internationale de Theatre de Jacques Lecoq still continues to develop and prepare students in the art of imaginative theatre collaboration.

When I tell students that Lecoq started as a gymnast, many of the group immediately think that I am going to get them leaping over boxes and working on parallel bars. I quell the fear in their eyes by reminding them of the original aesthetics of the Greek Olympic Games. It was the poetry of running that interested Lecoq at the age of 17 and the links between sport and theatre. The gesture and rhythm of sport was extended into his theatre practice, which he developed into a clear educational journey. My own physical training started every day, running slowly with extended movement in barefoot around a wooden floored hall for 5 minutes and then slowly going into a walk before finally standing in neutral attitude. It was not much fun to start with, probably because I felt out of my depth.

As I progressed, my movement technique slowly improved and I began to realise that I did not have to be great at sport to replay and create a dynamic piece. Lecoq offers a physical discipline that makes you aware of your own body's expressive potential in life and performance. I started to have fun in class when I just went for it. I am now mindful to recreate the enjoyment that I found during my process.

> I am a neutral point through which you must pass in order to better articulate your own theatrical voice.[2]

I frequently work with British A level students in Tolo, Greece. The process using chorus and tragedy is intense, culminating in an outside public performance. It is mirrored by an equally full-on social experience in a

Figure 3.1
Students warming up and working towards accurate movement. Annie is encouraging Sam and Kristian to enjoy focused work on each part of the body

holiday resort. Lecoq enables the students to move as one and tell a story with their bodies by going with the landscape rather than fighting against it. At the end of rehearsal, I often swim in the clear blue water of the Aegean Sea with the warm sun on my face. I use the memory of this sensation when I am back in London and I want to demonstrate a warm and happy gesture. I am still not a strong swimmer but push myself to my limit to move through the water with an awareness of my tempo and rhythm that I never had before. Recently a student said that he thought Lecoq was a bloke who wore masks a lot. In his book *The Moving Body*, Lecoq shares his teaching process in detail. I have tried to write this chapter by including exercises to help you understand some of Lecoq's movement philosophy and then exercises to use Lecoq when you are devising. These two sections follow the same journey, so you can practise each area separately or follow through as one unit. You have to practise your technique just like any other creative discipline before you can perform well, so I have included specific technique exercises and warm-ups in a separate section. Lecoq works towards preparation of the body, the voice, of the art of collaboration and imagination.[3]

Lecoq calls devising **geo-dramatics**. It makes sense if I remember that he links movement to nature and so teaches dramatic landscapes. When I write, I always try to structure my work as well as attempting to keep it

geo-dramatics
Movement linked to nature to make dramatic landscapes/theatre.

commedia dell'arte
Masked impro-
vised comedy,
originally from
Italy.

human comedy
Lecoq's style
of *commedia
dell'arte*.

playful and imaginative. Harlequin is a ***commedia dell'arte*** character, and balances both comedy and tragedy. These are two of the main styles that Lecoq explores, and his school uses an image of Harlequin as their tag. This chapter looks at **human comedy**. You can find exercises to practise tragedy in Chapter 4 on Berkoff.

BEFORE YOU START: WARM-UPS AND TECHNIQUE EXERCISES

43 PHYSICAL WARM-UP 1: ROLL AND STRETCH

Student exercise: roll up

- Stand in a circle and be in neutral, with your body open and relaxed.
- Move your head from side to side.
- Roll your shoulders and swing both arms.
- Bend your knees and roll your hips.
- Swing both legs and then bring your left leg up in front of you with your knee bent.
- Roll your foot from the ankle.
- Change leg.
- Repeat and push movement to its limit.
- Stand and bring your arms right up and stretched above your head.
- Drop them down as you bend over and collapse your body over your legs.
- Do this several times and focus on your breathing.

Notes for the student

Every actor has their own physical warm-up and you can build a sequence of exercises to suit your body, working towards breath control and accurate justifiable movement. The same applies for vocal warm-up. Lecoq sees the voice being thrown into the space[4] and should be warmed up as an extension of all movement (see Chapter 4 on Berkoff). These are a few basic exercises that Lecoq uses in his teaching.

Performance tip

Movement is never mechanical. I stand still and use Stanislavski to find the truth when I am blocked and my gesture seems forced. It is good to use other practitioners sometimes.

44 PHYSICAL WARM-UP 2: ENSEMBLE AWARENESS

Teacher-led exercise: all change

* Find a random position and stand in neutral.
* Start walking around the space.
* Stretch your body by visualising a piece of thread pulling you up from the top of of your head.
* Remember not to look up.
* Make eye contact with everyone as you walk round.
* Keep the movement light footed.
* Start running into the centre of the room.
* Keep moving and keep changing direction.
* Avoid touching each other.
* Move in and out of the centre and finish by seeing how close you can run together without touching.

Notes for the teacher

*Avoid walking in circles by saying 'change' regularly. Wait until the students can make eye contact without chatting and laughing before they run. The last part of this warm-up should be fun. When I am invited into a building to work with students, I always aim to get them moving within the first few minutes of a workshop. Warm-up games are well covered in other publications. I might start with a simple high energy game such as 123456. You can choose your own movement for each number, but I always use running from A to B, the dying fly (on your back with legs kicking), the cancan, and end with hugging someone. It is a good way to start the group listening and enjoying moving together. Then move into the focused exercises suggested above before walking. I will often start discussion while walking and ask questions as the group focus on moving around the space. Lecoq also includes **dramatic acrobatics**[5] in his warm-up and works on leaps, jumps, lifts, somersaults and falls to improve suppleness and strength. These are essential for clowning and comedy. Juggling is also used as part of the acrobatic technique. Other theatre companies and practitioners are brilliant in this area of movement. It is not my strength, so I recognise its importance and leave it to others. Lecoq would emphasise that actors should know their physical limits!*

> **dramatic acrobatics**
> Leaps, jumps, lifts, somersaults and juggling used in performance.

45 PHYSICAL WARM-UP 3: THE BALL

Student exercise: be ready

- Stand in neutral.
- Imagine a ball being thrown into the air and then falling down.
- Throw up an imaginary ball and then wait for a second before you bring your arms down to catch it.

Notes for the student

Lecoq is interested in that moment before the ball comes down again. It makes you open and ready as a performer.

46 TECHNIQUE 1: WITH ATTITUDE – STAGE ONE

Student exercise: move with the flow

- Stand in neutral and slowly go through all the attitudes.
- Remember to breath and keep your movement precise.
- You might want to start by moving with a **neutral mask**.
- Practise until your movement flows from one attitude to another.

Notes for the student

Use this technique with the neutral mask. When you push movement to its limit, there are moments of stillness. Lecoq devised a series of movements called **attitudes** to help students go beyond natural gesture. It can be used as a sequence to improve technique. Then experiment with different dramatic justifications and breathing just like the neutral mask. Figure 3.2 is a simplified version of Lecoq's sequence of attitudes.[6]

> **neutral mask**
> Used to make your body the focus of expression.
>
> **attitudes**
> A series of movements to help go beyond natural gesture.

Figure 3.2
Attitudes

47 TECHNIQUE 2: WITH ATTITUDE – STAGE TWO

Student exercise: justify

Once you are confident with the sequence you practised at stage one in the first section, you can add your dramatic justification.

- Try this simple sequence to practise.
- Remember to stay in one place and just move from attitude to attitude.
- I stand outside. I hear a noise. I turn around. I look. I am frightened. No one is there. What should I do?
- I move forward. I stand inside. I feel calm.

Student follow-on exercise

- Add a dramatic justification to each of the attitudes in the sequence shown in Figure 3.2. Here are some examples for the first five:
    - open/aggressive/strong
    - fear/pain (stomach)/insecurity
    - challenging/happy/loving
    - indecision/point of view (push)
    - indecision/point of view (pull)
- Think of your own dramatic justification. There are many possibilities for each attitude.

Notes for the student

As an actor, you can use attitudes really successfully when breaking down a monologue (see Chapter 4 on Berkoff). Then devise your own. I saw a brilliant installation as part of the Manchester Festival 2011, and it was a great comtemporary example of how this exercise can be adapted dramatically. Projected on to a wall was a film showing a single figure in 'generic army fatigues' moving continuously through exercises against a war-torn landscape. It was called *Infinite Freedom Exercise* by John Gerrard of Virtual World and choreographed by Wayne McGregor. It depicted a soldier's reaction to war. It was very powerful. You could easily add narrative, poetry or music and create an alternative way of staging an epic subject.

Performance tip

Keep the movement strong and simple when you are breaking up the speech into different attitudes. It changes the style of your performance.

48 TECHNIQUE 3: ACTING THE MASK – ADVANCED REVISION

Student exercise: express yourself

expressive mask

A full character mask with features.

- Use this technique with human comedy and **expressive masks**.
- Stand in neutral and isolate your neck by stretching it to the left and right, up and down.
- Then rotate your head around, keeping your mouth open as you tip your head backwards.
- Stretch your torso to the left and right, in and out.
- Stretch and flex your hands.
- Put your hands on your hips and roll your pelvis to the left and right, in and out.
- Then roll in a figure of eight.
- Stretch your lower face by yawning and pulling your mouth to the left and right.
- Now place a half mask on your face, and remember: *do not touch the mask*.
- Imagine you have one eye placed at the end of your nose.
- Examine the space by using the gaze.
- Imagine your mind is in your body and let your personality become the type of mask you are wearing.
- Walk around the room, being led by different parts of your body. Go to extremes.
- Let the mask do the work.
- Breathe from your gut.

49 TECHNIQUE 4: HUNGER

Student exercise: limb cuisine

- Think of your favourite food.
- Start obsessing about your favourite food.
- Back at the music hall, it is the interval.
- You are hungry and it has become desperate.
- You look at your limbs and suddenly they look tasty.
- Prepare and season your leg/arm as if you were suddenly on a cookery programme.
- Start eating your limb discreetly.
- It is delicious and you are starving. Push it to the extreme.
- Share your enjoyment.
- Try adding a red nose as the smallest mask.

Figure 3.3
Katriona wears a red nose
as the smallest mask and
makes her audience laugh
by taking the exercise
seriously

50 TECHNIQUE 5: PUSH AND PULL/ LOVE AND HATE

Student exercise: fronting

- In pairs, stand and face each other in neutral.
- Bring your left leg forward and your right leg back.
- Bend your left knee and put your weight forward on to that leg.
- Bring your arms up to shoulder height and place your hands vertically with palms up.
- Touch palms with your partner.
- Move backwards and forwards with your legs in a push and pull movement.

Figure 3.4
Push and pull

- Try not to travel; just change balance by straightening and bending the knees.
- When you have a rhythm, add the dialogue 'I hate' when you push and 'I love' when you pull.
- Think of a simple dialogue involving an argument, and decide who is pushing and who is pulling with each sentence.
- Say each sentence using the push and pull movement.

Notes for the student

There is no action without reaction.[7]

Lecoq uses the simple theory of *I love (pull)* and *I hate (push)* as the basis of all dramatic storytelling. If you extend it to *I am pulled, I pull myself* or *I am pushed, I push myself*, you can apply it to any character that you are playing. Ask yourself these questions when you are breaking down a piece of text or finding out the relationship between you and other characters. Use this exercise to get the action and reaction between characters and find their rhythm.

Notes for the teacher

Lecoq teaches this horizontal push and pull as the basis for clowning and particularly commedia.

Student exercise: a love and hate story

- Try acting this simple scene using the push and pull technique.
- I want to go out tonight. My mum will not let me. I push her away.
  I storm up to my room. My friends are waiting outside. They call me.
  Mum knocks on my door with a cup of tea. I take it. I decide to stay in.
  My friends tag the evening on Facebook. I want to go out tonight . . .

Notes for the student

Many of you will be considering applying to a drama school or university
where you will need to be self-motivated and expected to work hard. Treat
yourself to the best possible circumstances and you will allow your body to
be expressive and safe.

Space: You need it to move in, so leave your personal stuff in the corner.
Accessorise: Keep hydrated. Get into the habit of bringing bottled water to
class. Energy drinks are fine but bottled water is best.
Kit: Wear loose clothing, black or dark leggings and a T-shirt or tracksuit.
Every school has a sports kit. No changing facilities? Girls, bring leggings
and wear them under your skirts.
Bare feet are best.
Do not break the rhythm: if an exercise is difficult, resist escaping to the
toilet.
Breathe properly into your whole body. It helps to reduce tension and
possible injury.
Trust yourself and the other performers.

Figure 3.5
S. A. K. B. D. B. T.

Notes for the teacher

It is important to play on your feet by using the exercises practically. I appreciate that the demands of your timetable and facilities within your department sometimes make it really difficult to create the right time and space for movement-based work. Your space may not be perfect. If there is room to move around, it works. If the floor is clean and safe, then even better. Likewise, resist opening windows when the work becomes hot. It breaks the creative energy and also, from a health and safely angle, it could damage warmed up muscle. I always have a facility for playing music ready to go if necessary. I would include a session outside when planning this part of the specification. Lecoq's study of human comedy and human tragedy originates from two art forms that were performed outdoors. It can be the most valuable experience for students. I suggest starting with a warm-up, a technique and then an improvisation or a dramatic form.

UNDERSTANDING LECOQ THROUGH PRACTICE

51 IMPROVISATION: INDIVIDUAL

Student exercise: replay and play the silent way

> **AIM**
>
> To replay a situation silently and physically rediscover past images by using open mime and memory.

* Imagine a place that you think you have discovered for the first time.
* Stand at the door and take your time before entering into the space.
* You realise you have been there before.
* Rediscover the place and all the things in it.
* Nothing has changed.
* The images of the past become alive with each object you find.
* Something brings you back into the present.
* You leave.

Notes for the student

Lecoq sees mime as central to his theatre and not as a separate art form.[8] People still associate mime with Marcelle Marceau, who developed mime

Figure 3.6
Katrina is rediscovering
things in silence

as a silent individual performance in its own right. Students often start building walls in the air with their palms when I mention mime. By calling it **open mime**, Lecoq explains that he teaches mime as a human action to rediscover things you do in life and create them in another way. Open mime includes rediscovering objects as well. The gesture must have an emotional connection. Lecoq also uses **action mime** to look at our physical actions. I have suggested separate exercises for you to practise later on in this chapter. You can find exercises for other mime styles under the heading 'the language of gesture'. Lecoq starts his training in silence with simple improvisation. If you are comfortable as a group, then dive straight into the group exercises. It may be that you need to work on your own first, so you could start with this exercise. It is about memory. You can be anywhere and the present will remind you of the past. Lecoq looks at silent physical rediscovery. It is useful to remind you that improvisation comes from memory, whether real or imagined. Stanislavski uses similar exercises for actors using their imagination. This is more about physically inspired memory and is mimed.

Student follow-on exercise

- Practise miming objects on your own at home. Pick up a cup and feel its weight. You hold a cup of tea by its handle.

open mime
Central to Lecoq's teaching 'to play at being someone else and summon up illusory presences'.

action mime
To replay a physical action as close as possible. Also to copy the handling of objects.

Performance tip

When I played the wife in Steven Berkoff's *Greek*,[9] I was constantly picking up objects and then putting them down to see the tension and shape left in my hand. I found that the volume was really important and so was visualising the object to create the illusion. I drank tea in a china cup and extended my little finger out because the character thought she was posh. I needed to mime holding the saucer underneath for the illusion to work for an audience.

Notes for the teacher

Simon McBurney writes a great prologue about 'memory, people and remembering things' in Complicite's Plays 1,[10] *and all three plays in this collection are great for exploring Lecoq with text. If you want to study physical replay of memory, look at* 100, *devised by a company called the Imaginary Body.*[11]

52 IMPROVISATION: GROUP

Student exercise: group replay and play the silent way

AIM

To use psychological replay to improvise simple situations of life and work together in silence before words.

- Get your group moving together in the space (see Exercise 47).
- Choose one of these life situations and replay it together using your own experiences.
- Keep the space clear, with only minimal use of chairs.
- All objects are mimed:

    - cinema;
    - market;
    - coffee/cocktail bar;
    - college library; and
    - church.

Questions for after the exercise

- How do you play simple things?
- How do you manage to keep silent?
- Was there a temptation to mouth conversations?

Notes for the student

Most students can interact silently through social networking sites, and yet when they are told that they cannot speak somehow it becomes very difficult to avoid doing too much. Lecoq wants you to find out what goes on underneath the spoken language and is interested in the human silence before words are spoken. It is dramatically the most interesting. You will find a moment in the improvisation where you will want to speak. The silence after the words is not so interesting because Lecoq feels there is nothing more to be said.

Student follow-on exercise: the wait for Wills and Kate

- You have been invited to an afternoon drinks reception at Clarence House in recognition of all the fundraising you did for your local charity. It is not really your scene, but you are curious to meet Wills and Kate. You do not know anyone else who is going. The dress code is formal.
- Due to security, you have left all of your belongings in the cloakroom. You have been offered a cocktail just before you walk in through the door.
- You enter on your own, assuming that Wills and Kate will be there. The function room is empty. Other guests repeat the same process and arrive one by one. You all wait in silence because Wills and Kate might enter at any minute.
- They do not turn up.

53 THE NEUTRAL MASK

Teacher-led exercise: the eternal present

> **AIM**
>
> To 'be' in the present rather than 'act' and experience everything for the first time.

- Split into two groups, A and B.
- Group A, sit and observe Group B, who each hold a neutral mask.
- Group B, stand in neutral with your backs to Group A.
- Hold the neutral mask with both hands placed at the side of the face.
- Focus your energy by looking down into the inside of the mask.
- Place the mask on your face and move it until you feel comfortable.
- Adjust your hair if you need to, but do not use mirrors.
- Do not touch the mask during the exercise.
- Try to be in a moment of stillness.
- Slowly turn your head over your right shoulder and look out at the horizon.
- Let your body follow the movement until you are stood facing Group A in neutral.
- Group A give feedback then repeat the exercise with Group B observing.

Figure 3.7
The neutral mask

Figure 3.8
Group focus on the energy
of the neutral mask

Notes for the student

Work with the neutral mask is central to Lecoq's teaching. When you put on a mask, your face disappears and your body becomes your focus of expression. As an actor, you can experiment by moving freely in the space. You have to communicate through gesture and movement so it has to be specific and clear. The audience will look at your whole body and not just your face.

Student follow-on exercise: the awakening

- Group B, find individual spaces to lie down and relax.
- Wake up slowly as if it is the first time, and be aware of the space and how your body moves in it.
- Get up and explore.
- Repeat this exercise with Group A.

Teacher-led exercise: the farewell

- Stand and imagine you can see someone on the horizon.
- Wave to them.
- Try to attract their attention and play with different levels of movement. How big can you make your movement?
- You realise it is an old friend and they are leaving.
- Wave farewell.
- The sense of loss fills your body.
- You move on.

Performance tip

Experiment with breathing in and out as you slowly raise your arm to wave. It will change your intention.

Notes for the student

Spend some time discussing these exercises as a group. I remember doing a workshop with some students in Dorset who felt liberated because the audience cannot 'see you'. The students in the photographs were all really surprised at the power the mask gave them. Quiet students can become really strong performers when they wear a neutral mask. Because you are not playing a character, it is a really good way to find your own truth and balance as an actor. It is equally important to share what you saw.

Questions for after the exercise

- As an actor, how did you feel when wearing the neutral mask?
- When you watch the whole body, whose movement was clear and what level of gesture worked?
- How did you get up off the floor?
- Could you see emotion in the third exercise?

Notes for the teacher

These are three classic Lecoq exercises for the neutral mask. Lecoq used leather Satori masks, and they are undoubtedly the best for performance.[12] It would be a sound investment to buy a set of six leather masks, however they are expensive and may be out of budget. The plastic masks in the photographs were used originally in a production of The Trojan Women *and are painted with texture to appear less stark. You can customise them like commedia performers by building up the inside of the mask with sponge or foam to match the contours of the wearer. This would only work if each student had their own mask. Start your work with the technique found in the first section, called 'attitudes'.*

54 EXPRESSIVE MASKS

Student exercise: the mask finds a character

AIM

To work out how to play a character in a mask by using your body to communicate.

- Use large masks without human features, except for a big nose.
- Do not use mirrors.
- Move quickly into life.
- Split into Group A and Group B and take it in turns to project and perform.
- Group A, wear the masks and stand facing Group B.
- Group B, quickly project different situations on to the masks.
- It is happy. It is shy. It is horny. It is depressed.
- Group A, respond with the same physical level as the mask.
- Swap over.
- Give the mask activities.
- It is out clubbing. It is packing to go on holiday. It is taming a unicorn.

Notes for the student

When I was a student, I was a huge fan of Trestle Theatre. Their physical characterisation was painfully funny and honest. I auditioned for them once and was so nervous I forgot to breath in my mask. It was a good lesson, but I never made it into the company! Later, I worked as a practitioner with Joff Chafer, a founding member, and was reminded of the importance of play, especially when wearing an expressive mask. An expressive mask means a full character mask or a larval mask. It is not the same as the half masks used in *commedia dell'arte* (see Exercise 65 on human comedy).

Acting tip

In masked performance, your eyes are replaced by head and hand gestures (see Exercise 48 for advanced warm-up technique).

Notes for the teacher

Unlike the neutral masks, these exercises can be played quickly. This encourages students to get up on their feet and express themselves by thinking through movement. Try putting the larval masks into family groups and let them improvise sitting on a beach sharing a packed lunch or watching a DVD together at home.

Student follow-on exercise: the counter mask in three stages

- Look at the fixed expression of your mask.
- Put the mask on.
- Find a still image and take your body to the limit of expression.
- Think of some actions that go with the personality of the mask. Enjoy them.
- Then try actions that go against the mask and use more complex emotions.
- Then split into groups and work on one of the following improvisations that go against the fixed expression of the mask:
- You are in the corps de ballet and all are desperate to dance the swan queen in *Swan Lake*. The director's favourite gets the role and you must all congratulate her as he announces the cast.
- At a funeral, you get a message on your Blackberry saying that you have won the lottery rollover worth £10 million.
- You have to pack up your tent and leave the best weekend of the summer.

Notes for the student

How does a fixed smile look with acts of cruelty? The **counter mask** is the emotion that goes against what a character is visibly displaying – what a character is really thinking or feeling. The counter mask is useful to explore characters in conflict. Look at the technique called 'attitude stage two' in the first section as well.

> **counter mask**
> Playing against the emotion a character mask is showing.

55 CORE TECHNIQUE: ACTION MIME

Student exercise: vertical moves

> **AIM**
>
> To look at the main actions and movement of the body and put them into a creative context.

- Stand in neutral and keep your knees slightly bent.
- Work out a sequence of action that moves up and down.
- Use bell ringing or lifting a suitcase on top of your wardrobe to practise.
- Break down each stage of the action.
- Work out where your hands need to move and how that affects the rest of your body.
- Keep the movement economical.
- Start slowly and experiment with different tempo or speed.
- Remember to breathe.

Figure 3.9
Lifting

Figure 3.10
Bell ringing

Notes for the student

Remember that Lecoq always goes back to everyday life when you get confused with his method.[13] You have to practise your technique just like any other creative discipline before you can perform well. Think about your physical actions as being *vertical, horizontal* or *diagonal*.

Student follow-on exercise: country walk

Figure 3.11
Climbing a fence (adapted from figurative images drawn by Jacques Lecoq)

- Work out a similar sequence that moves across the space.
- Use climbing a fence to practise.
- Finally, think about a diagonal action such as throwing a javelin.

56 DRAMATIC CONTEXT

Student exercise: character action

AIM

To use action mime to tell a story.

* Choose one of the following characters:
    – Brontë heroine
    – Futuristic anti-government runner
    – British soldier in Afghanistan
    – Late night traveller

* Devise a sequence of vertical, horizontal and diagonal actions.
* Give them high energy.
* Think of the dramatic context.
* Give the character physchological reasons for the drama.
* Add specific music that puts the sequence in context with the character.

Notes for the student

Most of you will have access to an Xbox 360. I am not suggesting that you go home and exchange live performance for gaming. However, play *Mirror's Edge* (released November 2008 by EA) and think of how you could adapt this to practise action mime. The main character uses heightened action to overcome obstacles. Another media resource, of course, is film. Try *Run Lola Run* (directed by Tom Tykwer in 1998) for a good use of character and structure seen from different perspectives.

USING LECOQ WHEN DEVISING

This section can be used together with Chapter 7 to help you when you are devising a piece of theatre in a given style. If you have decided to devise your piece physically or use Lecoq, you can use these exercises within the structure of Chapter 6 on devising theatre. Remember to warm up and practise your technique.

57 IMPROVISATION FOR DEVISING

Student exercise: the waiting game

AIM

To replay simple situations of life in silence and use them within a piece of devised work.

- In pairs, sit and wait in silence:
    - on a sofa
    - on the bus
    - in the back seat of a car
    - outside an interview room
- As a group, wait in silence for:
    - a music festival toilet
    - school lunch
    - a self-service checkout
    - an Olympic gate entrance

Performance tip

These situations are purposefully simple and within your experience. Watch and be watched. Extend the pair work exercise further into a sequence of movement, which starts from this simple observation of our waiting lives.

58 THE NEUTRAL MASK AND DEVISING

Teacher-led exercise: journeys

AIM

To discover how nature makes you feel and move when you improvise journeys in a neutral mask.

- Walk round the room in neutral.
- Focus on deep breaths that fill the body.
- Walk in a calm and balanced state.
- Start your journey by walking over descriptive landscapes, rivers, mountains, deserts and forests.
- Walk, run and climb as you make your journey in a calm and balanced state.

Notes for the student

You might want to go back to the exercises on the neutral mask to practise being in the present first. Lecoq strongly identifies with nature and so does the neutral mask. These exercises allow you to experience wearing the neutral mask to move forward and advance by making journeys through landscapes and the elements. It is not just the journey you make as a character that interests Lecoq. How do you journey from A to B in performance but, more importantly, what happens along the way?

Devising tip

You could use this exercise as another way to show your character's journey in your piece.

Notes for the teacher

Each student should wear a mask and improvise alone, even though this is a group exercise.

Student follow-on exercise: your reflective journey

- Sit and think about your emotional response to different landscapes.
- By linking your feelings to movement, try to share a poetic response to your journey.

Figure 3.12
Journeying through
landscapes

- How did your breathing change and affect your response?
- How did wearing the neutral mask help?

Teacher-led follow-on exercise: stormy weather

- Walk around the room in neutral.
- Start journeying through hazardous landscapes.
- Make sure you use your body fully and travel to your limit.

Notes for the student

Lecoq wanted students to experience the extremes of nature and connect with their deeper feelings. You could use this either to help with playing a character or to devise an abstract response to different moods created by moving through landscapes. The ball technique is a great warm-up for this work.

Student follow-on exercise: identification – earth, wind and fire

- Choose one of the four elements: earth, wind, fire or water.
- Play with *being* the wind of the storm or the water of the sea.
- In your group, apply the following instructions to your element:

  - Face the sea.
  - Watch it.
  - Breath in and start to breath in the movement of the waves.
  - You gradually become the sea.

Figure 3.13
Earth, wind and fire

59 POETIC JOURNEYS

Student exercise: *el viento es un caballo*

> **AIM**
>
> To use text as stimulus and devise a group piece using movement as
> a poetic response.

- Get into groups.
- Look at one of the short extracts of poetry taken from *The Captain's Verse*, written by Pablo Neruda.[14]
- Devise a short piece using images from the text.
- Think about the work you have been doing on journeys and elements.
- You can use the neutral mask or move without it.

Wind on the Island

The Wind is a Horse	*El viento es un caballo*
hear how he runs	*oyelo como corre*
through the sea, through the sea	*por el mar, por el cielo*

The Mountain and the River

Night climbs up the mountain	*La noche al monte sube*
Hunger goes down the River	*El hambre baja al rio*

Notes for the student

The reason for this work is to look at the poetic substitute for a character you might be playing. For example, you might have a hot temper with the qualities of a raging fire. Your character might be weak with the qualities of wet seaweed. Once you are confident that you can express yourself physically, take the neutral mask off.

Notes for the teacher

The Voyages of Sinbad, *translated from the original* Arabian Nights,[15] *are great for journeys. Many of Brecht's plays have journeys, and I would recommend a text such as Complicitie's* The Three Lives of Lucie Cabrol *as perfect stimulus for devising.[16] Students can devise in abstract, create their own epic stories or use journeys for character development. Start with the earlier exercises on the neutral mask, otherwise you could have problems getting them to take the* **identification** *work seriously. I worked with some students in East London and they found it easier to start with recognisable urban materials (see Exercise 60 on urban ID). Never ask the students to be a tree! Lecoq made actors work at the tree because he wanted them to achieve a balanced body, rooted in the ground.*

> **identification**
> Finding a character by physical identification with materials and elements.

Devising tip

Try this exercise by using the lyrics of a song that fit your theme.

60 URBAN ID

Student exercise: city life

AIM

To identify with materials and find a character.

- Here is a list of urban materials:
  - crumpled magazine cover
  - low-battery iPhone

- flat energy drink
- freshly ironed shirt
- melting chocolate bar
- ripe banana
- light-hold hairspray
- microwaved porridge

- Choose one.
- Stand in neutral.
- Think about what sort of breath and rhythm it might have.
- Start with a still image of your chosen material.
- How does it move?

Notes for the student

Lecoq uses identification of materials to find a character just like colour, animal and sound. Discuss what sort of people would fill your urban landscape if they were all, say, ripe bananas! This exercise will help you find your chosen character or characters within your devising piece. Think about an urban material that fits your character.

61 CHARACTER SWAP

Student exercise: inner beast

> **AIM**
>
> To identify with animals and find a character.

- Choose a character you have played or will be playing.
- What animal are they?
- Be still and silent as the animal you have chosen.
- Which gesture?
- What movement?
- Move around the space.
- Give your chosen animal human speech.
- Now return to a still image of the character you have chosen.
- Get two chairs and sit down in pairs.
- Improvise a simple dialogue between your two characters.
- Choose moments to let your animal out.

Student follow-on exercise: colour ID

- Use the same character.
- What colour are they?
- Suggest movements for this colour.
- Think of the shade and light of the colour.
- What rhythm is it?
- Share your work and see if the group can guess what colour you are.

Notes for the student

Lecoq encourages students to work on character identification by using nature, animals and colour. It is quite hard to describe things through movement if you are not used to this way of working. Just go for it and try to let it come from your own body. You do have to connect emotionally. Be careful. Recently, I did a workshop with some A level students, looking at their version of *Brontë* by Polly Teale.[17] The students were quite reserved, and we unlocked some explosive emotion when we identified with the Brontë sisters! Leave enough down time after this exercise.

Student follow-on exercise: identify your moving world

- Look at the movement in your favourite paintings or illustrations.
- How would you describe them through movement?
- Move and compare graffiti to the pre-Raphaelites.
- Next time you dance to your current iPhone track, listen to the music and get into the deeper movement of the actual sound.
- Does it push or pull you physically (see Exercise 65 on human comedy)?

Notes for the student

You can extend the work into what Lecoq calls a 'universal poetic awareness'.[18] Remember, he teaches that 'a better understanding of what moves' helps you have 'a better understanding of what movement is'.

Devising tip

Finding the movement of a word can completely change how you say a line of text.

62 EXPRESSIVE MASKS AND DEVISING

Student exercise: passing the emotion

AIM

To explore levels of emotional playing.

- Sit in a line.
- Start at one end of the line and pass on the emotion by turning your head and looking at the person sitting next to you.
- When you reach the end of the line, pass it back down the line rather than starting with the first person again.
- The emotion should pass up and down the line and the level of emotion should increase as each person passes it on.
- The first emotion is *cheerfulness*.
- Move on to *gloom*.
- Stand in a line and do exactly the same with *irritation*.
- Move on to *fearful*.

Notes for the student

It is important, as an actor, to explore your emotional range. Lecoq encouraged his students to push their emotions to the limit. Remember to start your emotion in the body. Some styles of theatre require a high level of expression. When rehearsing a naturalistic drama, it is still useful to explore how far that character could go emotionally before finding the right level of performance. You might need only a small and simple moment, which can be just as powerful.

Figure 3.14
Passing the emotion

Notes for the teacher

The students in Figure 3.14 found that they could push happiness to its limit easily. They found it more difficult to get angry with each other, so group dynamic is really important. This exercise is simple and exposing. It shows how devising groups need to trust each other.

Performance tip

A few years ago, I worked with a group of students from Brighton on *The Trojan Women*. They were a really chilled ensemble and it was not until they pushed grief to its limit that they could really get to the intensity of the piece. Sometimes, the other end of the scale can be equally as moving in performance. Look back at the work you did on memory in Exercise 51 on improvisation and Exercise 57 on improvisation for devising.

Devising tip

This exercise can be a perfect way to revitalise and re-energise during the devising process. At any point, if you feel like you are losing inspiration, run this exercise as a group and then go back to the scene you were working on.

63 STORYTELLING AND EXPRESSIVE MASKS

Student exercise: expressive brain storming

AIM

To experiment with contemporary expressive masks to tell stories.

- Dress your mask in everyday clothing, including hats and hair extensions.
- Make your own fashion mask.
- Experiment with practical masks that are used in real life (e.g. builders' masks, sunglasses, sports masks).
- Multiple role play using several actors playing the same character mask.
- Character chase: one actor plays two characters chasing each other by changing mask and costume behind a screen.

Notes for the student

Creative work must be of our time.[19]

If you are studying the Edexel translation of *Lysistrata*, then I would really push you to use masks at some point in rehearsal (look at the exercises in

Figure 3.15
Male students, Kristian
and Joseph, join Shelley
as part of the female
Greek chorus

Chapter 4 on Berkoff). Masks work particularly well with the chorus of old men and women. Download some traditional images of older Greek women. Try tying black headscarves around the masks and work on strong gestures to match. Put them through domestic activities such as scrubbing the floor and carrying water. Role reversal makes your interpretation more interesting (see Figure 3.15). I worked with a group of students who were studying the play and had set it during the Second World War. When they put masks on the Women's Institute, who were abstaining from sex, they found the comedy.

Performance tip

Check that everyone is playing with the same physicality and level of emotion. If you do not, then the audience will think that either you or your group are in a different play to everyone else.

64 THE LANGUAGE OF GESTURE

Student exercise: dumb show pantomime

AIM

To look at different types of gesture and mime to tell stories.

- In groups of five, look at the following extract from *Hamlet*. Re-tell the story using gesture alone to replace words.

Hamlet by William Shakespeare. Act 3, Scene 2

The dumb-show enters. Enter a King and Queen, very lovingly; the Queen embracing him, and he her. She kneels, and makes a show of protestation unto him. He takes her up, and declines his head upon her neck; lays him down upon a bank of flowers; she, seeing him asleep, leaves him. Anon comes in a fellow, takes off his crown, kisses it, and pours poison in the King's ears, and exits. The Queen returns, finds the King dead, and makes passionate action. The poisoner, with some two or three Mutes, comes in again, seeming to lament with her. The dead body is carried away. The poisoner wooes the Queen with gifts; She seems loath and unwilling awhile, but in the end accepts his love. Exuent.

- How hard was it to keep the storytelling clear and the movement economical?
- Did any of the students in your group over-use their facial expressions?
- How would objects or costumes aid the story?

Notes for the student

You have already practised open mime in the improvisation exercises on replay and play the silent way and worked on action mime. This exercise is to show you how limiting **pantomime** can be. It is a style that uses hand gesture, and sometimes it is tempting to replace every word with a gesture or a facial expression. This is known as 'mugging' in the theatre, or basically just pulling faces.

Notes for the teacher

It is worth sourcing the film Les Enfants du Paradis *for the classic example of Pierrot brilliantly played by Jean-Louis Barrault.*

> ## Performance tip
>
> I have a very animated face and really have to be careful to keep it relaxed. Your face and body need to express emotion, but do not try to have a physical 'conversation'.

Student follow-on exercise: three perspectives

- Go back into your groups of five and look at the *Hamlet* extract again. Perform the story using three different visual perspectives:
- Inside the action (the person actually giving the action, e.g. the poisoner pouring into the King's ear).

> **pantomime**
> Where gesture alone replaces words; associated with white pantomime/Pierrot.

- Outside the action (seeing the action from another perspective, close up, from a different scale, e.g. represent the poison pouring into the ear).
- Commenting on the action (communicate the emotion of the action with gesture, e.g. another actor shows the poisoner's cunning not by playing sneaky, but with gesture).

Notes for the student

This exercise is using **mimage** and basic **cartoon mime**. 'Mimage' is a word that Lecoq used and is just what it sounds like: a mix of mime and image to reveal how the character is feeling. It is just a quick flash to show the audience a character's inner state. It can be shown by the actor playing the character or other actors in the scene. It is a great style of storytelling to break out of naturalism.

Student follow-on exercise: movie night

- At home, think of your current favourite movie. How would you recreate the opening sequences of your film using cartoon mime?
- Try to include the three different perspectives. Here are some suggestions:

   - *Chariots of Fire* (Hugh Hudson, 1977)
   - *Star Wars* (George Lucas, 1977)
   - *Titanic* (James Cameron, 1997)
   - *Kill Bill* (Quentin Tarantino, 2003–2004)
   - *Invictus* (Clint Eastwood, 2009)

Notes for the student

How could this style be used in a piece of devised work?

Lecoq encouraged his students to recreate whole films on their own, using his techniques to tell the story. Today, the use of film image, video and installation is very popular in theatre. Knee High Theatre used original film footage of *Brief Encounter* and also recreated moving images. When you are working with mixed style and media, it is important to make sure the storytelling is still clear.

> **mimage**
> A zoom into a character's internal feeling.
>
> **cartoon mime**
> Peformed like a silent movie of images.

Devising tip

If your group decides to use film footage within your piece, make sure you think through how and where to project images for maximum effect on the audience.

Notes for the teacher

The language of gesture enhances performance, and Lecoq wanted his students to have a vocabulary of gesture to use in devised work and with dramatic text. See the glossary for definitions of different mime styles.

65 THE DRAMATIC TERRITORIES: HUMAN COMEDY

Student exercise: extreme passing the emotion – stop, you are killing me

AIM

To explore some areas of human comedy originating from *commedia dell'arte*.

- Stand in a line.
- Choose either laughter, desire, hunger, love or jealousy.
- Start at one end and pass the emotion from one person to another.
- Give the person eye contact and increase the level of emotion each time.
- Pass back down the line until it is so painful that you actually die from the emotion.
- Go through each emotion.
- Push to the extreme and discover the fear.
- Find a space and stand on your own.
- Are you Pantalone or Harlequin?
- Use the following scenarios to explore changing from one extreme emotion to another in a couple of seconds. Start with one and then decide on a reason to die of another and then move on:

  – Harlequin's takeaway dinner.
  – Pantalone's birthday present.
  – Harlequin's new shoes.
  – Pantalone gets a text.

Notes for the student

Lecoq was very influenced by *commedia dell'arte*, and uses many of its key features in his teaching. The movement is based on animals, and the characters are types, usually masked. Even if you have not studied *commedia dell'arte*, it is useful to know the two main characters, Harlequin (the servant) and Pantalone (the master). Remember that Harlequin has quick, precise movements and that Pantalone is an old man. Your eye at the end of your nose is called the **gaze**.

> **gaze**
> In *commedia dell'arte* the end of your nose becomes your eyes.

Performance tip

If you have long limbs or an uncoordinated body, use it to heighten the comedy like a performer called Dario Fo who collaborated with Lecoq.

Notes for the teacher

I think that the most useful book for more detail is Commedia dell'arte: An Actor's Handbook *by John Ruskin.*[20] *Lecoq preferred to use the term human comedy. All the earlier work on animals is great for this style. Let the students have fun. Use any of the plays by Dario Fo for exploration of text, particularly* Can't Pay Won't Pay. *The exercises are a variation of his Zanni sketches. Give the students the opportunity to perform outside; it will make a difference.*

Teacher-led exercise: status hierarchy and the fly

- Give the students the following information:

  The 1870s was a golden time for London East End musical hall. Both the acts and the audience are great social groups to divide into character status to explore human comedy. Starting with the highest, the following acts had clear status or billing rank in the show:

  1 comic character singers
  2 the *lions comiques* (swaggering young men)
  3 female impersonators
  4 male impersonators
  5 speciality acts

  - ventriloquists
  - jugglers
  - magicians
  - cyclists (Kaufmann's cycling beauties)
  - trapeze

  6 adagio acts (dancers)

- Ask the students to decide on a character and work individually on their physicality.
- Let them line up in order of status.

- Ask the group to match energy levels and decide on the hierarchy.
- Sit down together and give the students the following information:

  The company has been called on stage for a publicity photograph. You must find a group pose. While waiting for the photographer to set up, the company must stand still. Imagine a fly buzzing around you. It flies in front of each character. Each character must notice the fly as it lands on them and then must get it off them without moving. Keep eye contact with the fly so that the audience can clearly see its journey.

Notes for the student

Start quite small and let the fly go around the whole group once. Add the buzzing sound. What happens when the group get rid of the fly collectively? Lecoq explores the main commedia plot themes of hunger, love and money. Remember these three stages: the story, what to play and how to play. I am showing how you could devise a piece using the same story structure. You could use anything from Bollywood to the Welsh valleys as long as the characters remain traditional and stock mask types.

Performance tip

Push your character to the extreme and reveal the fear.

Notes for the teacher

Feed in extra information, such as in commedia – the zanni who is a low status servant is always hungry. You could move the situation back into the scene by shouting 'smile' at any time and maybe more than once.

Student follow-on exercise: star-crossed lovers (love)

- You are at the music hall theatre sitting in a box with your family.
- Your lover and their family are sitting in a box opposite.
- The show is over and both families leave their boxes.
- You both keep coming back for one last compliment.
- Neither can say goodbye.
- You just cannot exit.

Notes for the student

The lovers in commedia are usually star-crossed like Romeo and Juliet and never masked. Their moves are very light footed and almost balletic. Think of two doves. This exit speech is called a chiusetta.

Student follow-on exercise: push and pull (money)

- Improvise the following in the style of human comedy. Wear half masks if possible. Keep the moves sharp and highly energised:
Backstage during the show, things are kicking off. It is Saturday night and the wages are ready. The comedy singer is missing so the stage manager gives the money to an adagio dancer to give to the comedy singer. The adagio dancer gives the money to the trapeze artist to put in the comedy singer's dressing room. The wages are left in the wrong dressing room and are taken by the magician, thinking there has been a pay rise. The comedy singer has been performing in several music halls around the East End to make more money. The comedy singer is late and sends a message via the trapeze artist. The trapeze artist has not eaten since the matinee and is really hungry so forgets to deliver the message when food arrives. The magician is accused of stealing the money and the adagio dancer, who loves the trapeze artist, tries to sort it out. The manager has just seen the comedy singer perform at another music hall and has rushed backstage to demand the money back. The show is still on.

66 LECOQ'S CREATIVE QUESTIONS

Student exercise: essential ingredients

AIM

To explore Lecoq's creative questions.

Here is a perfect checklist when using Lecoq as a practitioner for plays or devised work. It is a simplified version of his own structure. As the bloke using masks said, '*toute bouche*', or 'everything moves'.

> *toute bouche*
> Everything moves.

- What risks are being played for?
- What parts of human nature are used in melodrama, comedy or tragedy?
- How are you behaving and how does that affect your movement?
- What powers the drama during these forms of theatre?
- What is the most effective style or language for expressing these risks? Half masks? Real objects? Chorus?[21]
- How do they work and can they work together?
- What plays or dramatic texts do you use to explore these territories?

Tell us a story.[22]

Devising tip

Sit down in your group as you get towards the end of the devising process and go over these questions, using your responses to feed into your drama.

SUMMARY: LECOQ

As an actor, you can observe the movement of life and replay silently.

Be with the drama = the neutral mask
Be for the drama = the expressive mask
Be against the drama = the counter mask

There is no action without reaction, so:

- **Horizontal** action mime is the push and pull of drama, or the me and you, or the love and hate.
- **Diagonal** action mime is the emotional levels of drama.
- **Vertical** action mime is the poetic heaven and earth of drama.

Be playful in the theatre of movement and imagination.

See the drama in form or style.

Start telling stories with **dramatic territories**:

- Horizontal = human comedy or clown.
- Diagonal = melodrama.
- Vertical = tragedy or reverse bouffon (see Chapter 4 on Berkoff).

Lecoq uses the image called the rose of effort to illustrate his influence.

Sport movement and theatre combined together in Paris when Lecoq watched a performance of Jean-Louis Barrault, who played a man and horse moving as one.

Antonin Artaud also became a friend.

Lecoq worked with Jean Daste, who had been a student of Jacques Copeau in France.

Lecoq used their ideas of using silent theatre (*pantomime blanche*), *commedia dell'arte*, **Japanese Noh theatre** and Greek tragedy to understand the extremes of acting.

With Daste, he discovered masked performance, with all the actors wearing neutral masks.

dramatic territories
Key dramatic styles such as comedy and tragedy.

Japanese Noh theatre
Stylised classical Japanese dance drama using character masks.

Back in Paris, he wanted to create simple theatre using both mime and voices.

Remember that Lecoq never trained in mime, and his school today studies all forms of movement, including the discipline of what he called action mime.

Lecoq really discovered *commedia dell'arte* first hand in Italy. At the University of Padua, he met the sculptor Ameleto Sartori.

Sartori reproduced the original leather masks of *commedia*.

Lecoq was taught character movements and gestures, and started teaching how internal emotion and external movements should be extreme by using *commedia* masks to work on breathing and exercises to 'scale up' the emotion.

At the Piccolo Theatre in Milan, he collaborated with Giorgio Strehler and Dario Fo to create political physical comedy.

Lecoq also developed his own interpretation of Greek tragedy at Piccolo, and this became part of his teaching.

In 1956, Lecoq returned to Paris and opened his school, where the main training structure is still known as 'the journey'.

Companies and collaborators to look out for

Theatre of Scotland
Complicite
DV8
Kneehigh
Frantic Assembly
Horse and Bamboo
Peta Lily
Nola Rae
Robert Lepage
Steven Berkoff
Volcano
Punchdrunk
Peepolykus
Spymonkey
Company of Angels
Bootworks,
Gandini Juggling
1927
Toby Sedgwick (2012 Olympic Games Opening Ceremony)

4 Berkoff
(1937-)

If I have a trademark style, I suppose it's about physicality, simplicity of communication both orally and physically. That's very important.[1]

Steven Berkoff was born in Stepney, London and is still an energised actor, playwright and director. Berkoff trained as an actor at the Webber Douglas Academy in London and studied movement at the Ecole Internationale de Theatre de Jaques Lecoq in Paris. These two disciplines are key to his creative work. Berkoff eloquently records his life and creative journey as part of his published work, so I will not insult him by attempting a mini biography in this introduction. I would recommend that, as students, you at least read *Diary of a Juvenile Delinquent*,[2] which is what it says on the tin. It is an informative insight into the young Jewish man growing up in the East End of London. It will definitely feed your understanding of the poetic violence and excitement found in some of his verse plays. In 1968, Berkoff formed the London Theatre Group and, like another influential actor/director, Laurence Olivier, proceeded to write, direct and perform with his own company as well as appearing in iconic films of the period. 'Yeah, Annie, but he can't still be alive?' asked a student recently after he had enjoyed sweating as Gregor Samsa in Berkoff's adaptation of Kafka's *Metamorphosis*. I think that the reason Berkoff is so relevant to young people today is the fact that he is still hungry for creativity. In 2011, he performed *One Man*, which included two of his one-man shows, *Dog* and *The Tell Tale Heart*,[3] which he adapted from Edgar Allen Poe. It was just him on stage, and he is still the best example of his own actor-based theatre. Berkoff's voice can also be heard in a major PlayStation 3 game[4] and he often appears in current trending films. He was 74 in 2011 and is actively involved in current contemporary culture. So yes, Berkoff is still alive and well. Of course, there are new generations of artists exploring contemporary non-naturalistic theatre. However, unlike any of the other practitioners in this book, you really can go and see his work first hand. Berkoff can be dismissed as the *enfant terrible* he relishes in playing, but you would be underestimating his vast knowledge. Berkoff's work is influenced by Greek theatre,

NB

Japanese Noh and **kabuki**, Shakespeare, East End music hall and his Jewish heritage, as well as using the techniques of practitioners such as Artaud and Brecht. His own actor training would have included Stanislavski, and the techniques used by Lecoq are vital if you are going to practise Berkoff's work properly. The use of mime, stylised movement, exaggerated vocal work, direct asides and improvisations within an ensemble environment are all key features.[5] I have focused on the use of **chorus** and ensemble in his adaptations, looked at his East End roots in some of the verse plays and written exercises on how to use his style with text.

As a performer I find Berkoff's work challenging. I know and respect the man himself, as well as many of the actors within his core ensemble. A good friend of mine was recently part of the *Oedipus* ensemble. During the play, the chorus action mimed a happy gesture. Having worked with him in Greece, I sat in the audience, and knew immediately that his gesture was from the same sun-kissed Aegean Sea that I described in the introduction to Chapter 3 on Lecoq. Never forget that Berkoff is a style that must be based in truth.

There are many ways to reach Nirvana.[6]

kabuki
A classical Japanese dance drama with elaborate face make-up.

chorus
A non-individual group of performers found in Greek drama who comment together on the dramatic action, both vocally and physically.

Figure 4.1
Annie and Shelley are stretching as part of their warm-up for Berkoff's style

UNDERSTANDING BERKOFF THROUGH PRACTICE

67 THE BASE PULSE

Student exercise: feel the breath

base pulse
The rhythm and ensemble movement used in choral work.

AIM

To understand how to use the **base pulse**.

- Stand in neutral with your knees slightly bent and arms by your side, making sure that your body is open and centred.
- Keep your head out front and as if wearing a neutral mask (refer back to Chapter 3 on Lecoq for help with the neutral mask).
- Start with your left foot and slowly transfer balance from your toes to your heel, bringing your weight down gently to the ground.
- Visualise a redistribution of energy flowing from one side of the body to the other, and do the same with your right foot.
- Keep the toe/heel rhythm going for a couple of minutes.
- Make sure you are keeping your head up and your body open in neutral.
- Concentrate on the definition of movement between the toes and heel.
- Now get into a group of at least four.
- Choose one person to stand in front and use that person as the leader.
- Stand in neutral and take your rhythm from the leader.
- Do not look down or at each other.
- Start to work in time with the leader and each other.
- After a few minutes, as you all start to work in rhythm together, you will have found your group's base pulse.

Notes for the student

This exercise is all about finding the choral pulse of your group. This is in preparation for when you will work on stylised movement as an ensemble. It is the basis of all Greek choral work and is another of Lecoq's main dramatic territories.[7] You may find that, as a group, you start to work in time with each other fairly easily and establish your group base pulse almost organically. This exercise is always good to come back to, as a group, to warm up and harmonise.

Figure 4.2
The base pulse

Performance tip

When I was rehearsing Berkoff's *Greek*, I had never worked with the three other actors before. We were very different energies, however this exercise found our performance pulse.

Figure 4.3
Annie is reminding the group to really flex the heel and toe. Shelley is going to lead the base pulse

68 THE GREEK CHORUS

Student exercise: the tragic story

AIM

To understand the use of chorus in Berkoff's work and how it relates to ensemble playing.

- Get into groups of five.
- Find a space and stand in a square with four distinct corners.
- The fifth student should stand in the middle.
- Make sure you have enough room to move with both arms extended.
- Number your corners.
- If you are student 1, stand at a diagonal and tell the other students to turn their bodies to stand facing directly behind you.
- Student 1, you are the first leader of the exercise.
- Student 1, start using the base pulse from the previous exercise. After a minute, keep the base pulse going and add the following sequence:

  - Stretch your right arm up and extend it right through to your fingers.
  - Stretch your left arm up and do the same.
  - Stretch your right arm to the side.
  - Stretch your left arm to the side.
  - Move both arms around in a circumference.

- Remember to breathe.
- Turn 90 degrees slowly to the right so that the group is standing behind student 2.
- Keep the base pulse going and the movement flowing.
- Student 2 is now leading.
- Repeat the sequence until all four corners have led.
- Student 5 should swap with a corner to practise leading.
- Once you feel confident as an ensemble, you can be more adventurous with your arm gestures.

Notes for the student

Make sure your energy extends to the end of your fingers and you keep your arms strong and energised. Do not lose the beat of the base pulse, and work on keeping your focus during the exercise. I always say to students

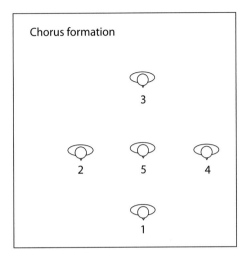

Chorus formation

Figure 4.4
Chorus formation

that, if you cannot see anyone, then you are leading. Most students admit they feel nervous about this and many cannot believe that the chorus are still moving behind them. Trust when you are leading, and try not to be a diva when you are following. It is important that everyone has a turn at leading. Lecoq saw a Greek chorus being made up of fifteen actors, with one leader and either one group of fourteen or two groups of seven following. Try this exercise with this formation and experiment with balancing the stage in different formations.

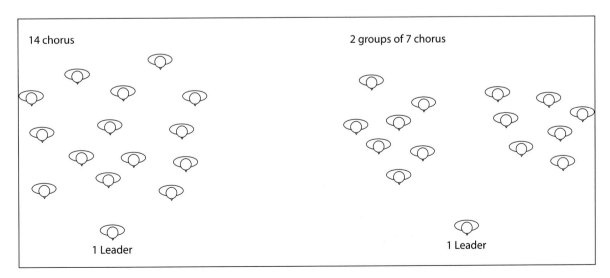

14 chorus

2 groups of 7 chorus

1 Leader

1 Leader

Figure 4.5
Two-chorus formation

Student follow-on exercise: *march sur place*

- Go back to the base pulse and keep your arms by your side.
- Keep your head up and focus on a chosen point out front.
- Slowly extend your left arm out to reach your right knee and your right arm out to reach your left knee as if walking on the spot.
- If you slowly extend your legs out behind you as if speed skating, then you can try running on the spot.
- Remember to stay together as an ensemble, allowing the rhythm to guide you.
- Whenever you feel that you are out of time with the others, just follow your leader and allow the rhythm to draw you in.

Questions for after the exercise

- What was your individual focus like?
- When, as a group, did you feel you were together with the pulse and when did you feel you lost it?
- When you were moving as one, did you feel more focused as a group?
- How would you describe the ensemble experience?

Notes for the student

Berkoff's early work is based on classical Greek texts and contemporary modern day verse in an ensemble environment. In Greek theatre, the chorus used to be played by a group of male actors trained like athletes. Berkoff often uses the chorus in a stylised sequence of movement, usually heightened both vocally and physically. Just like a traditional Greek chorus, they reflect the mood of the story and express what the main characters cannot say. His chorus can be the family in *Metamorphosis* and *East*, or a chorus of old dockers playing pigeons in his stage adaptation of *On the Waterfront*. In 2011, he reworked his original adaptation of *Oedipus*, and some of you may have seen it at the Edinburgh Festival. The first exercise is just the start of working together physically as a choral ensemble. The ***marche sur place***,[8] or walk on the spot, is also great for individual storytelling. Berkoff uses several walks, including his signature heel/toe walk used as characters enter a scene.

> ***marche sur place***
> A stylised way of walking on the spot.

Notes for the teacher

I really recommend that you include some of the techniques and warm-ups found in Chapter 3 on Lecoq to get the most out of Steven Berkoff's work. His style is influenced by his own training. Likewise, Greek tragedy and the use of chorus is a major territory in Lecoq's dramatic journey. Remember the rose of effort where all vertical movement relates to Greek storytelling connecting the gods in heaven and the humans on earth. Often, teachers are surprised when I start a Berkoff workshop with Greek choral exercises. This is a focused and pure exercise to demonstrate Berkoff's demand for physical and emotional communication. If you refer back to the work on mask in Chapter 3 on Lecoq, you can easily add an emotion to the exercise and push the chorus to its limit. For example, if you add the emotion of 'grief', then already the exercise moves into the Greek tragic chorus. Do not be discouraged if the students start laughing when they get into the sequence of the pulse. Some students can find themselves quite exposed and start sending up the moves. Expect some streetdancing or even a breakout of 1970s dance moves. Just remind them to keep it slow, maintain their focus and connect with the others in the group. I find students understand what working as an ensemble is like when the pulse is working and they are all moving in time. Once they have discovered this, they usually strive hard to re-find it when they lose it.

69 BOUFFON

Teacher-led group exercise: making a mockery

AIM

To look at the mocking role of the **bouffon**.

- Feed the group the following information:
  Bouffons are like a chorus because they are a group of performers. They usually move in a gang of five. Unlike a chorus, they are physically **grotesque** and have no opinions.[9] Bouffons have fun by mocking humans and society. They are never individuals, but always big collective movements, such as war, or themes, such as religion. They see and play with everything.[10]
- Look together at contemporary cartoons that mock politicians and compare them with some of the images of William Hogarth, the eighteenth-century painter.
- Ask the students to draw their own bouffon with exaggerated physicality.
- Now ask them to create their bouffon physically.
- Encourage the use of padding to emphasize the bouffon's extremities.
- Walk around the space and have fun.
- Get into a gang of five bouffons.

bouffon
Performance style used by Lecoq drawing on mimicry and the grotesque.

grotesque
A fantastic and outrageous element of bouffon.

- Look at the following list of themes:
    - politics
    - religion
    - economy
    - power
    - money
    - morality
    - war
    - gender
    - or decide on your own theme

- Make fun of your chosen theme by moving as a gang of bouffons.
- Let your bouffons reveal the truth of your theme.

Notes for the student

cryptos
The Greek meaning of 'hidden'.

Bouffons are a mix of Greek chorus and clown. Grotesque is also called ***cryptos***, which in Greek means 'hidden'. The bouffon reveals what lies beneath the drama. Lecoq uses this dramatic territory in his teaching. Berkoff often uses this group in his plays, and an audience can be uncomfortable with a bouffon piece when they reveal the truth of humanity. Because they are grotesque, they can be funny, so that can be difficult if they are mocking serious social themes. Berkoff uses bouffons to reveal

Figure 4.6
Gang of bouffons

greedy rich Jews in *Messiah* and to mock war in his version of *Coriolanus* by William Shakespeare. Berkoff's group of bouffons are violent and drunk in sections of *Greek*.[11] Bouffons are a great way of using a thought-provoking theatre style.

Student follow-on exercise: gangs of bouffons at play

- Get into groups of five.
- Choose one of the following groups:

    - farmers in a Soho bar
    - nuns at Reading Festival
    - gardeners in a skateboarding park
    - Greek widows on a beach
    - fairies in a graveyard
    - IT geeks in a field

- Work out a sequence using the bouffon style of performance.

Performance tip

If you want to include a bouffon sequence in your piece, it is useful to have one item of costume that is worn by the whole gang. An obvious choice, for example, is bowler hats if you are mocking money and bankers.

Extra technique: the seven ages of man

- Start curled up on the floor like an unborn baby safe in its womb.
- Think about moving forward physically to show the main stages of man in a sequence of movement (Figure 4.7):

    - birth
    - baby
    - toddler
    - child
    - teenager
    - professional
    - mature
    - senior
    - death

- Try to lead your movement with your head.

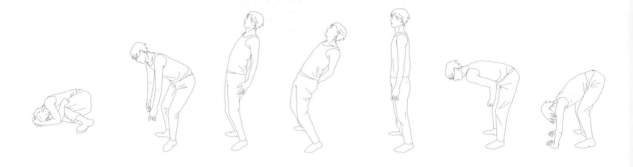

Figure 4.7
Seven stages of man

- Keep the movement fluid and simple.
- Go back into the womb.
- Think about what you were like as a child, how you are now as a teenager and how you imagine your life might move forward.
- Do the exercise again and spend time on physically exploring each stage of your life.
- Include mime to indicate what you might be doing.

Student follow-on exercise: are we human?

- Start curled up in the womb.
- Think of a character you are playing.
- Add a piece of music, such as 'Human' by The Killers (there is a point in the lyrics where they sing 'cut the chord', which is a great cue to be 'born').[12]
- Repeat the seven stages and physically move forward as that character.
- Include mime and think of the environments you might be in.
- Take your time.

Notes for the student

This is a version of a classic Lecoq technique. When I do this exercise with students, they are amazed at what they discover about their physical lives. Characters move the drama forward. As an actor, you need to decide on their back story. Sometimes this is within the text and sometimes you have to create it yourself from what you know about the character. By exploring his or her journey through movement, you can make a character's physical life clear. Even though Berkoff's work is played in a heightened reality, you still need to make truthful decisions as a performer. For drama geeks, the title of this technique is taken from Jaques' famous speech in *As You Like It* by William Shakespeare.

Student follow-on exercise: understanding the burden

- Most of the characters in Berkoff's plays are burdened by personal guilt, inactivity, unfulfilled promise or opressed by society and its conventions.
- Think of a character you have played or would like to play.
- What is their burden?
- Think about how you could show this physically with the use of *action mime*.
- In character, gather up your burden and carry it around the space.
- It is heavy and overwhelming.
- Your burden weighs you down.
- You try to get rid of it but it just will not go away.
- Lie down on the floor, exausted by your efforts, and relax.
- Sit in a circle and share what you thought your character was burdened with.
- How would this influence the playing of this character?

70 THE SPOKEN WORD

Student exercise: kvetch

> **AIM**
>
> To explore the muscularity of the spoken word.

- Find a space and sit on the drama studio floor.
- Think about the last time you moaned about something.
- Turn around to the person sitting next to you and have a good moan.
- Now put your moan or complaint into a five-line structure.
- Try to get the tone of your moan in the words you use.
- Emphasise the words that illustrate this most.
- Use exciting and rich vocabulary, even if your moan is quite ordinary.
- Allow yourself to experiment vocally with volume and tone.
- Stay truthful.
- Stand in neutral and focus out.
- Work the muscles in your face before you start.
- Luxuriate in saying your moaning speech out loud. Start to project your voice and enjoy the new rhythm you have found.
- Now share your **kvetch** as a piece of vocal storytelling. Directly address your audience.
- Find the person you originally moaned to.

> **kvetch**
> Taken from a Yiddish noun and means to complain all the time, usually with humour.

Figure 4.8
Sam is expressing his lust in a heightened style

- You are sitting eating dinner.
- Try to chat about your day.
- You both cannot resist the need to moan in this heightened style of performance.

Student follow-on exercise: love and lust

- Find a space and sit on your own.
- Think about a person that you adore.
- Do you love them or fancy them?
- Your love or lust could be unrequited (secret or not returned).
- Put your feelings into seven sentences.
- Make your description rich with exciting and dynamic vocabulary.
- Try saying your love or lust speech out loud by focusing on a chair.
- Focus and use the chair as the object of your desire.
- Allow your speech to be filled with the truth of how you feel.
- Be passionate and physical with your language.
- Now share your passion with the audience while remembering to explore the pace at which you describe your passion and using the tone and volume of your voice.
- Replace the chair with another student and ask him or her just to stand in neutral as your reference point so you can maintain the intensity of your speech.
- Concentrate on the spoken word, as we will be adding movement in the next exercise.

Notes for the student

In the next exercise, we will add movement to the spoken word. Berkoff uses love and lust as a vital dynamic for his dramatic work. It can be teenage sex, fantasy and disappointment like *East* or it can be beautiful like Eddie's speech in *Greek*.[13]

Performance tip

Berkoff's theatre style can be exhausting to maintain both physically and mentally. Try this for a quick refocus back into the ensemble and away from naturalism: stand in a circle and assume the position of a sumo warrior. Shout *sumo large*. Bring your bodies up into neutral and offer your arms out to the group, palms up and say *sumo love*. All the students that have been part of my process know that this is my signature. It works for us.

71 EAST END SPORT

Student exercise: keeping it real

AIM

To explore the muscularity of the spoken word with a contemporary created character.

You are Mobile Danny and provide the estate with a tidy little service. As it happens, you are stood outside White Hart Lane on a Saturday afternoon hoping to enjoy the North London derby. You have already been stressed up the Caledonian by two gooners and your smart juice is low. Plus, you do not really want to hang in riot territory. When Proper Dave shows up with his missus instead of your mate, Slaphead Tony, who owes you a ton, you do not want to kick off in front of the lady, but something needs to be said.

Pav the Turk has a gym on the Forest Road. You are Wifi Calvin and go there on Monday, Wednesday and Friday mornings before you graft for Garage Lil. You always nip over to Pizza n Chicken for a cuppa with a Lucozade on the side and a plate of chicken and fries. You take your favourite seat in the cafe and you know you look pumped up and peak. The waitress is a hot spice and you always enjoy flirty banter. When your order arrives, the tea is too milky and the chicken is cold. You are torn. You want to complain to Delphine but you want to shine in her eyes. Plus the fact her old man, Two Motors Mas, is the owner.

- Choose one of these back stories and read it out loud.
- Take your time to enjoy the language and make it energised.
- Get into a group and improvise the scene.
- Avoid making it too naturalistic by using techniques such as action mime and attitudes found in Chapter 3 on Lecoq.
- Keep the physical and vocal levels high but do not rush or shout.
- Be specific.

Student follow-on exercise: monologue

- Find a space and reread the two improvisations on your own.
- Imagine you are one of the characters re-telling the story.
- Write a monologue spoken by the character you choose to play.
- Keep to the same story structure found in the improvisation.
- Do not be afraid to use a mix of street and more old school vocabulary.
- Read each sentence out loud.
- If it does not sound energised, then change it.
- Try to keep the storytelling raw and truthful.
- Listen to the rhythm of the speech.
- Stand in neutral and experiment with the sounds of the words you have written.
- Break the speech up into sections.
- When you are happy with the vocal story, you can add physical technique such as gesture or attitudes as before.
- Really enjoy re-telling your character's story.

Notes for the student

Berkoff's characters use a mix of poetic language, sometimes Shakespearean, often vulgar and muscular, almost physical. Lecoq saw speech as an extension of movement and taught students to imagine throwing their words out into the air. It is a good image when you think of this style. Berkoff also manipulates sound through language. Remember to keep the energy levels high, while fully embodied and based on the subtle truth of your emotion.

Do not be afraid to be sexual or contemporary in your dialogue as well as the odd classical phrase. Street slang can be mixed with poetic beauty, but try to avoid shouted and uncentred speech. Berkoff wrote *East* when he was a hungry and angry young actor (read his book, *Diary of a Juvenile Delinquent*). He also wrote *East* and *Greek* in verse. At the end of *East*, Berkoff includes a list of East End slang. As you know, the nature of the street changes almost daily, as does fashion, music and trending. Here is some fairly recent vocabulary that might help you:

- spices – girls
- rave – party
- blud – friend
- link – come
- don't act shook – don't be scared
- nuff – lots
- peak – good thing
- shine – do well
- sick – great
- competition – battles
- burnt – losers
- moves – your weapons on the dance floor

Before you look at the fight exercise, read the fight scene between Eddie and the manager in Berkoff's *Greek*. At first, it just looks like a list of great-sounding words. If you read it out loud, then you will find a carefully crafted fight sequence ending with Eddie killing the manager. Have a go at your own now.

Student follow-on exercise: fight

- Reread the first exercise, 'keeping it real'.
- Get into pairs.
- Choose to be either:

  - Mobile Danny and Slaphead Tony outside White Hart Lane; or
  - Wifi Calvin and Two Motors Mas in the cafe.

- Improvise an argument.
- Use language that is muscular and descriptive.
- Let the argument build until you reach your limit.
- Do not shout.
- Break your text down into five lines each.
- Now choose seven words each.
- Stand in front of each other and throw each word as if you were physically injuring your opponent.
- React with a sound after each blow hits you.
- Take each word and sound to its limit.
- Experiment with the pace and rhythm of your argument.

- Work out a series of action mimes to go with the words.
- React physically as well as vocally to each wound you receive.
- Practise and try not to laugh.
- Move away from each other and face out to the audience.
- Imagine your opponent is in front of you and repeat the whole sequence.

Performance tip

When the two actors playing Eddie and the manager were rehearsing the fight sequence in the production of *Greek*, they played with all the classic styles of fights such as Kung Fu, westerns, samurai and world war. The more graphic and heightened you can be with the words, the better. When we were on tour, the fight got a round of applause every night.

Notes for the teacher

This section specifically looks at the language derived from the East End. If it is not possible to study some of the explicit language used, then you could apply the same techniques to Berkoff's adaptations of Oedipus *or* Salome. *The language is rich and written in a contemporary version of classic verse. You could explore the poetry and epic style of storytelling in the same way.*

USING BERKOFF WITH A TEXT

In this section, I have used Berkoff's adaptations of *Metamorphosis* and *The Trial* by Kafka. These exercises can be used to apply Berkoff's style to any text of your choice. Unlike Stanislavski and Brecht, Berkoff will often start his rehearsal process by going straight into scene work. In this chapter, I have mirrored how Berkoff would work to enable you to structure your rehearsals in a similar way to create the Berkoff style of **total theatre**. Within the student notes and teacher notes, there are pointers to help you adapt these exercises to the text of your choice. I have also included a summary of rehearsal tips to help you at the end of this section.

total theatre
Performance with equal elements of movement, text, visuals and music.

72 CHARACTER, MOTIF AND GESTURE

Student exercise: finding the *mie*

AIM

To explore the physicality of Berkoff's characters by focusing on his version of *Metamorphosis*.

- Look at the opening stage directions of *Metamorphosis*.
- Focus on the family characters of Mr Samsa, Mrs Samsa, Greta and Gregor (before he becomes an insect).
- Decide which character you are drawn to and find a space on your own.
- Think about the detail of your character's physicality and what they are wearing.
- Make decisions from the information you are given in the stage directions.
- Stand up in neutral.
- Find a pose for your chosen character.
- Your body should be energised and in a state of alertness.
- Think about the detail and precision of your pose.
- Use your whole body and not just your face.
- Your pose, or *mie*, must be heightened and non-naturalistic.

Notes for the student

Steven Berkoff is influenced by a Japanese style of theatre called kabuki. This is a highly stylised classical dance drama, and you can find examples of it on YouTube. In this style of theatre, **mie** means a picturesque pose to establish your character. It is a great way of putting your character immediately into the Berkoff performance style. Steven Berkoff first played Gregor Samsa at the Roundhouse in London in 1969. In his book *Meditations on Metamorphosis*, he talks about how he was a salesman like Gregor and how he travelled each day from his family home in a north London council block. He used his own experience to find the character of Gregor.[14] In 1976, he played Mr Samsa at the National Theatre, and this time looked at old photographs of his grandfather as a starting point. Remember, it is important to start from the truth of real life and then move into Berkoff's style of performance. Berkoff saw Mr Samsa as a parody of all father figures and decided to play him like a human cartoon. Look back at some of the exercises in Chapter 3 on Lecoq to help you.

mie
A character pose using a heightened physical style.

Student follow-on exercise: finding the gesture

- Move around the space as your chosen character.
- Think about the shoes you would wear and how that affects your physicality.
- Stop and stand in your *mie* pose.
- If you are using *Metamorphosis* as your text, then add the following character motif or gesture:

  - Mr Samsa: light and smoke a pipe.
  - Mrs Samsa: peg out the washing from a basket.
  - Greta: play the violin.
  - Gregor: read an open newspaper.

- If you are using another text, use the same process, then:

  - Think about an action or gesture that illustrates what your character does within the play.
  - It could be something your character yearns to do or simply what they are seen to do in the play.
  - Build up a sequence of movement using the character *mie*, walk and motif.
  - Add a drumbeat or a piece of music from Puccini.

Notes for the student

In the opening sequence of *Metamorphosis*, the family use character motifs to move together and represent a beetle. This is one of the play's abstract images. Think about your text and a strong image that your ensemble could create by using the techniques of *mie* and motif. I worked with three students who used Berkoff as their practitioner with *The Maids* by Jean Genet. They decided that deceit and disguise were key elements in the play, then worked on an opening sequence using a character motif of dressing and undressing both as maids and Madame. By adding a piece of string-based classical music, they created a powerful and visual introduction to the play.

Notes for the teacher

It might be useful to share Kafka's original short story with the students before you look at the text. I would do this with any text you decide to use. Kafka's story is told from Gregor's room and the family are in the background. Explain that Berkoff reversed this by having the Samsa family telling their story in a heightened reality, with Gregor's progress being reported like a Greek tragedy. Immediately, they will see how his style of theatre is used while honouring the original writer's story. The students need to remember that Kafka's vision of Gregor, the condemned man, still needs the intensity of playing as well as all the technique explored in the exercises.

After a vocal and physical warm-up, I usually ask the students to sit in a circle, turn and face out and then lie down on their backs in a relaxation position. If I feel they need focus, then I ask them to shut their eyes. I usually sit in the middle and tell them the story of Metamorphosis. *If it is a large group, then I will also read out the opening stage directions. This way, they are still active physically and are not safely sitting in their chairs holding the text. When they are in their first poses, make sure that all the body is active. Usually the hands and feet need to be stylised. You will probably find a space full of Gregors. That does not matter for this exercise. In single sex schools and colleges, I have met the best physical representations of Mr Samsa by female GCSE students, and recently I worked in Croydon where Greta was played beautifully by a male Year 13 Drama student.*

This section is a template for using Berkoff with a text. I have applied these exercises to his Kafka adaptations, particularly Metamorphosis *because it demonstrates some of his total theatre style. This does not mean that you have to use these texts. Recently, I worked with some female students using a version of Berkoff's* Agamemnon. *We used the same process, and they found it particularly useful to distinguish the male and female characters that they were multi-role playing.*

Performance tip

As an actor, I was lucky enough to play Greta, and I used to hold a pencil as my violin bow during every rehearsal until I got the precision of my action mime (see Chapter 3 on Lecoq). I still had to work on my character, as well as my technique, so that I could understand the intensity of Kafka's story.

73 THE FAMILY AS A CHORUS

Student exercise: family deconstruction

AIM

To tell a story through ritual and heightened reality using the characters in *Metamorphosis*.

- Put a row of four chairs side by side.
- Place as many family groups of four chairs as your class needs.
- Decide which family character you are playing.
- One person, sit in a strong *mie* pose for every row of chairs.
- Remember to push the physicality to its limit.
- Do not forget your feet and legs.
- Without talking, try to add the three other members of the family group.
- Join the first person and sit in your character's *mie*.
- Be generous, and change your choice to fit the family of four if there are too many of one character.
- Try to create a strong physical representation of the family.
- When your group is ready, get up and stand in neutral in front of your chair.
- Individually, work out three clear moves that will deconstruct how you sit down and achieve your final character pose.
- Stand in neutral again, then all four characters move together with their individual deconstructions.
- Look out as if wearing a mask.
- Walk in a line as actors and stand in neutral in front of your chairs.
- Repeat the same character moves as before.
- Share with the other family groups.

Questions for after the exercise

- Which *mie* worked best for each character?
- If you paused the deconstructions from neutral to sitting, would there be a clear visual image at every moment?
- Was there a sense of the family moving as a chorus of individuals?
- How would this style affect the way the characters spoke the text?

Notes for the student

When you all walk on as the family and stand in front of your chairs, remember the base pulse exercise where you all felt the movement of the ensemble. Recently, I was in Sidcup working with some Year 13 students who entered, stood and sat as the family by listening to the rhythm of their chorus and sensing the other performers. They really used what they had learnt earlier. Berkoff's attention to detail can seem boring if you are not used to this style. Sometimes when I do this exercise, the students shout at me 'not again'! When you work on a piece of text using Berkoff's style, you have to treat both the words and movement like a precisely choreographed piece of theatre. There should be room for improvisation and play, but you have to find the stylised physicality to understand his work properly.

> I wanted to exercise the possibility of an actor being stretched beyond the pale of naturalism.[15]

Look back to all the techniques in Chapter 3 on Lecoq. They will help you achieve the skills required. Remember, his stage directions can sometimes be a scene themselves. If you think of the family as a Greek chorus, then that should help with your storytelling. You can use this process with any of Berkoff's texts.

74 ENACTING THE CEREMONY

Student exercise: family breakfast

AIM

To practise the rituals enacted within the drama and explore the **jo-ha-kÿ** style of performance.

> **jo-ha-kÿ**
> Stylised classical Japanese dance drama using character masks.

- Sit in your family line of chairs as the four Samsa characters.
- Think about what your character eats for breakfast.
- Be very specific. For example: What cereal? What bowl? What type of spoon?
- Imagine there is a long table in front of you.
- Start eating your breakfast using precise and heightened action mime.
- Remember to stay in character.
- Keep your face up and out to the audience.
- Take the best five moves and make the eating more of a ritual.
- Keep repeating the same five moves.
- Add the ticking of a clock or a metronome beat.

Figure 4.9
The students are in the early stages of improvising the family at breakfast. At the moment, their movement stops at the waist so it is not truthful and they lose their characters' physicality and attitude

Notes for the student

Berkoff uses both Lecoq and kabuki theatre styles in his work. When he uses the family chorus in his plays, they all enact the rituals of their domestic lives. The Samsa family and the families in *East* and *Greek* either go to the pub or sit around the table for a meal. In his latest production of *Oedipus*, all the ensemble sits around a table like the last supper. Look at the text on page 83 in *Metamorphosis* and notice how the dialogue is in a rhythm.[16] The short sentences suggest the anxious state of the family. In the play, Gregor is still in his room, however it is useful to do this exercise with all four characters at the breakfast table. The actor playing Gregor can adjust his focus to being late for work. Domestic ritual is important for any character that you are playing. This exercise is useful even though there may not be a meal scene in your chosen text.

Student follow-on exercise: high anxiety

- Look at this stage direction from page 83 of *Metamorphosis*:
  The mime of FAMILY eating, looking up, wondering where Gregor is, in unison linked as a chorus.
- Sit back at the breakfast table and recap on your five moves from the previous exercise.
- Play the track 'Colourbox' by Philip Glass.[17]
- Start eating normally as before.
- Remember to keep the mime heightened and sharp.
- Add the movement of looking up and wondering where Gregor is.

- Become anxious and agitated so that the repeated movement is very fast.
- Do not lose your character *mie* and the clarity of your mime.
- Slow the eating sequence right down and really stretch out your movements.
- Keep all your body active, and not just your arms, hands and face.
- Show the audience your worry by keeping your face out.
- Experiment with different energy levels.
- Share the sequence with the other families.
- Look at this stage direction on page 84 of *Metamorphosis*:
  The ticking stops suddenly – the silence accentuates the stillness – their world of eating and normality ceases. They move now in very slow motion beginning to show anguish.
- Link the two short extracts together to create your version of the family at breakfast.

Questions for after the exercise

- All you have done is decided what your character eats for breakfast and played it in a theatrical style. How could you apply this style to other text or devised work?
- Did you feel the intensity of the scene?

Notes for the student

The kabuki concept of *jo-ha-kÿ* is common in Berkoff's work. Scenes are done at a certain pace; the action is slow, speeds up and ends quickly. This Japanese concept governs actions of actors and structures of plays and scenes. To break it down further, **jo** is a slow and auspicious beginning (the way Berkoff often introduces character and plot), **ha** speeds events up (Berkoff often uses this and culminates the story with a moment of tragedy) and **kÿ** is a short and satisfying conclusion (many of Berkoff's characters move on quickly after tragedy).

You can also link with Artaud's use of ritual and his influence from Bali, which also interested Berkoff. *Jo-ha-kÿ* is a great way to look at a text and the rhythm of storytelling. It can release the style from naturalism.

Notes for the teacher

I always place my family rows in a large square so that the students can share the work without moving around and losing focus.

75 THE MINIATURE STAGE

Student exercise: bohemian rhapsody

AIM

To use the actors as part of their environments and take their expressions to their limits.

- Get into groups of five.
- Two actors, stand on a chair facing out in neutral.
- Two actors, stand directly in front of them facing out in neutral.
- The fifth actor, clap the rhythm.
- Work out a sequence that just moves the head to the extreme left, right, up, down, etc.
- Move the eyes in the same way.
- Include a beat where all four heads look out to the audience to express extreme emotion.
- Have fun.
- Think of the Samsa family in *Metamorphosis* and add the characters' expressions to your sequence.

Notes for the student

There are several choral focus exercises that you can do together, and the isolation warm-up in Exercise 48 in Chapter 3 on Lecoq is also a good way to work towards ensemble precision. It is quite hard to keep moving as one and maintain your individuality. Berkoff is interested in your body telling the story as well as a 'beefy' way of speaking the text. Try to find a mask-like expression for your face so that you really work your body. Obviously, the exercise title is taken from Queen's song and the band's cult video. It is important to have fun with the text and keep it fresh. Like any physical practitioner, Berkoff takes inspiration from film, and Akira Kurusawa movies particularly. Check out the 1971 film adaptation of Anthony Burgess' *A Clockwork Orange* by Stanley Kubrick, where a young Berkoff can be found. This iconic film, with its controversial content, is a brilliant example of this theatrical style of playing.

Student follow-on exercise: fear and loathing on a chair

- Find a chair.
- Imagine this is your miniature stage.
- Using all of your body, experiment with running, walking and your daily routine, all from a seated position.
- Try expressing extreme fear or joy using all of your body, but remain seated.
- Get into groups of four and place three chairs in a row.
- Three actors sit as the family group of Mr Samsa, Mrs Samsa and Greta.
- Find your character *mie* and sit in a high-level state of fear.
- Work out a sequence using the head movements from the previous exercise to include:

  - listening for the chief clerk;
  - showing the audience how you feel;
  - responding to each other reacting to the arrival and entrance of the chief clerk; and
  - following him as he walks around the room.

- The family must remain seated, and all reactions are physical.
- The fourth actor enters the scene as the character of chief clerk.
- Stand with high status, either left or right of the family, in a character *mie*.
- Move around the room with authority.
- Look at the stage direction on page 85 to help you with the mood:
  The FAMILY shrink back on their chairs – freeze in attitudes of fear and oppression by authority represented by the CHIEF CLERK.

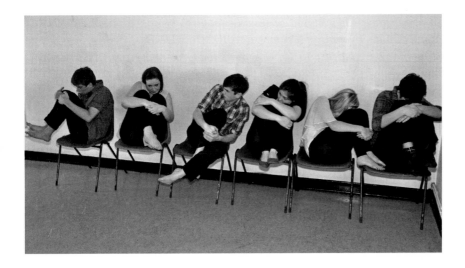

Figure 4.10
The group start using their chairs as a miniature stage to express their emotions

Performance tip

Use the Lecoq exercise called 'passing the emotion' to help you find the level of performance. You should be centred and warmed up properly to do this work safely.

Notes for the student

Berkoff decided to use three stools for the family to enact out many of their domestic rituals. He staged Gregor behind them in his 'room'. Berkoff wanted to make the actors work in a theatrical way that still showed them functioning as a family. He saw the stools as miniature stages that meant that the actor could not hide in the naturalism of a normal set.[18] Chairs can be a great springboard for non-naturalistic theatre or epic storytelling. Sometimes, I go into colleges and they have very limited resources. Students talk to me about their plans for complicated sets using screens or flats and endless lists of properties and furniture. By using chairs as your miniature stage, you immediately have another acting space. I was in Wales with a group of students working on Harper Lee's *To Kill A Mockingbird*, where we used chairs as verandas. Characters could sit and drink tea at the same time as characters in jail below them or break into a chase using techniques from this exercise. Add some strong lighting and you can create dynamic theatre scenes with minimal set.

Notes for the teacher

When I rehearsed Metamorphosis, *we had trouble getting the stools the right size and shape. They should be secure enough to be able to move quickly and at maximum physicality. It can be a really strong devise if done properly, and it enabled the audience to see Gregor as a chorus and protagonist staged in reverse.*

76 ON TRIAL

Student exercise: warm up with unspoken crimes

AIM

To look at specifics of Berkoff's version of *The Trial* and use it in the rehearsal process.

- Stand in neutral.
- Yawn and stretch the face as if someone is pulling your skin in all directions.
- Get into groups of six.
- Individually, think about what a chief bank clerk's worst crimes could be.
- Discuss them as a group.
- Think about the guilt of doing nothing.
- Choose an actor to play Joseph K.
- Stand in neutral in a strong chorus position.
- Joseph K should start by facing the chorus.
- The chorus continuously open their mouths as wide as possible and then shut them.
- This should be done silently.

Figure 4.11
Students standing in a circle when you do a vocal warm-up to check levels of style

- Joseph K hears all of his worst crimes and reacts silently.
- Change actors and start thinking about the audience and style.

Student follow-on exercise: warm up with punctuation

- Stand in neutral and breath in and out.
- Start humming.
- Visualise humming through your stomach, your chest and your head.
- Place your hands on each area and try to focus your voice.
- Say the following sequence of punctuation marks:

  Full stop comma semi colon full stop. Exclamation mark. Comma comma full stop. Question mark. Full stop full stop comma comma full stop.

- Make sure you end your words crisply and precisely.
- Repeat the sequence quickly, then slow it right down.
- Get into groups and devise your own choral punctuation soundscape.

Notes for the student

Recently, I have been visiting schools and colleges where several drama departments use Berkoff's version of *The Trial* as their text. These simple exercises are just tasters to show how you can link everything to his style of working. One school in Reading had made heavy frames to represent the doors in the play. It was not until I came and worked with the group that they realised that the frames needed to be light so that the chorus could move them about. Berkoff's own introduction is very clear[19] about creating environments using the chorus, and it seems that most students understand this style. I sometimes play Gargoyles and Angels as a warm-up where you quickly have to become gargoyles or angels individually, then gradually build into groups, and finally the whole group should build the cathedral. This is another good way of keeping your process within the context of the play.

Student follow-on exercise: strip mime

- Find a space on your own.
- You are in your bedroom.
- Mime taking your clothes off ready for bed.
- Be precise in your action mime and take each garment off slowly.
- Once you have got a sequence, start again.
- Imagine you are a cheesy magic show act and show the audience each item of clothing as if it was an amazing trick.

- Flirt with your audience and have fun.
- Now become the character of Miss Burstner in *The Trial*.
- Imagine you are wearing long gloves and old fashioned stockings with a big bra and petticoat.
- Make your **strip mime** theatrical.
- Try adding classic music tracks such as 'Je T'Aime . . . Moi Non Plus', made in 1969 by Jane Birkin and Serge Gainsbourg.

> **strip mime**
> A style used in clowning and pantomime (see Chapter 3 on Lecoq).

Notes for the student

Sex in Berkoff's plays is often a sequence of clowning deriving from his Lecoq training. For this reason, I suggest avoiding current popular music at this point. Rihanna may be a sexy recording artist, however avoid recreating a music video. Try reverse gender too. Classic tracks found in the 1997 film *The Full Monty*, directed by Paul Cattaneo, such as Donna Summer's 'Hot Stuff' or 'You Sexy Thing' by Hot Chocolate, might make you groan, however they are great for this kind of work. You could have a chorus of men playing women and then men and so on. Remember that the chorus of old men and old women in *Lysistrata* by Aristophanes all take their clothes off in front of each other. This is a perfect opportunity to use strip mime. Many of Berkoff's characters are sensual and explicit, however there is never the same full-on sex often found in contemporary naturalistic drama. Look at Sylv's speeches in *East* or the wife in *Greek*. Berkoff balances this with poetic love and beauty. When Salome mime strips in a dance it should be an exquisite and delicate piece of theatre. This is an extension of the ritual and ceremony explored in earlier exercises.

Notes for the teacher

Steven Berkoff is a great admirer of Lindsay Kemp and recalls going to see Kemp's Pierrot enact a bawdy and very funny strip mime at the Hovenden Theatre Club in his book Meditations of Metamorphosis.[20] *Berkoff's texts are often considered as too risky to be studied because of their perceived vocal and physical explicitness, and I know many drama teachers feel safer with* The Trial *and* Metamorphosis. *I do think you need to look at a Greek adaptation, an East End piece and a Kafka interpretation to get the full measure of Berkoff's work, however I also appreciate the pressures within your own building. So, to reassure the critics, I would say that all Greek theatre had scenes of trauma, violence, sex and catastrophic events that were committed off stage. It is the telling of these terrible stories by the messenger that moves the audience. Shakespeare uses the same devise and so does Berkoff. Berkoff thinks that art should have no limits and that stories should be told with total theatre skills to move an audience and not make them voyeurs.*[21]

SUMMARY: BERKOFF

If you are working on a Berkoff text or using Berkoff's style with another text, then try this rehearsal process:

– Start with a warm-up from Chapter 3 on Lecoq.
– Learn or refresh a technique from Chapter 3 on Lecoq.
– Go straight into any of the exercises found in this chapter.
– Divide your session between ensemble work and detailed character work.
– Only read the text together when you have found your group ensemble and at least your character's *mie*.

Sometimes, Berkoff uses one-to-one sessions with his actors to work on a scene, and sometimes he will focus on detailed choral sequences.

If you are doing two heavy sessions of physical work, make the next session vocal work on monologue and language.

White face paint is useful to enhance the total physical style of performance. Berkoff often uses this in his work, although not in his recent productions. It is not specific to Berkoff, and is rooted in both Greek tragedy and Lecoq-based performances.

Avoid trying to impersonate the actor Steven Berkoff. He is unique. Use this chapter to understand his style.

> To make the actors a fundamental part of their environment, to use every actor on that stage to the maximum of their ability and to express something to the utmost of its potential – sometimes literally, sometimes symbolically – so you can go no further with it.
> If anything, that's what they'd call the Berkovian Style.[22]
>
> Steven Berkoff, February 2009

PART 2

Skills you will need

5 Rehearsing a monologue/ duologue

This chapter is designed to take you through rehearsing a monologue or duologue from the first reading through to your final run. Rehearsing and performing a monologue or duologue has different demands from those of rehearsing a play. This chapter will walk you through how to tackle this, whether it is part of your A level course, for LAMDA acting exams, or those all-important drama school auditions.

Your first task is always to choose your monologue and duologue. There are an incredible range of books designed to help you choose (some of which are listed in the further reading section at the back of this book) so we will not look at choosing in this chapter, apart from saying that you are not just going to choose a speech to say out loud, but rather a character to create and experience. So choose a character you enjoy from a play you like and go from there.

Probably the first thing I notice when watching a monologue or duologue is whether the student has created a truthful and believable character based on a set of given circumstances or if they are 'busking it', having learnt their lines and hoping that will be enough to see them through. I often start watching a monologue, and after a few lines of dialogue I can usually tell how much preparation the student has done. Your character may only be on stage for 2 to 5 minutes, but you need to do the same work as if your character is on stage for 3 hours.

In a monologue or duologue, we see a snapshot of a life on stage, and the audience should be left understanding the character who lives that life. To do this, I have designed this chapter to take you through this process. This chapter is how I teach monologues and duologues, and is a collection of exercises that I have found to work well. So, once you have chosen your piece, start with the first exercise and work your way through, timing your work so that you reach the last exercise a couple of days before your exam or audition takes place.

The exercises from Chapters 1–4 on the practitioners will help you to rehearse and perform your monologue or duologue if you decide to use a particular practitioner's influence to enhance the work you do in this chapter. For those of you preparing for the higher LAMDA medallions who need to link to a practitioner, this chapter uses a largely Stanislavskian structure. When combined with Chapter 1 on Stanislavski, it will fully prepare you for your exam. Those choosing Brecht can use this chapter in conjunction with Chapter 2 on Brecht.

It is worth remembering that, when performing a monologue or duologue, the audience will just sit and watch you act. There is nowhere to hide on stage, and if you do not do all the work needed to create a character, this will become clear to your audience very quickly.

I have created a number of detailed exercises within this chapter so you have all the tools you need to rehearse and perform a strong monologue and duologue. Now it is over to you . . .

77 CONTEXT OF THE PLAY

Student exercise

> **AIM**
>
> To understand the context of the play from which you have chosen your monologue or duologue.

- Find a quiet space and read the play from start to finish.
- Think about your character and what your character is like.
- Jot down your first impressions of what the play is about, what your character is like and what you think the playwright wanted to tell the audience through the play.

Notes for the student

It is important that you read the whole play before you finalise your choice of monologue or duologue. Remember, you are acting out a piece from a play, and it will be the knowledge you gain from reading the play that will help you start to create your character. If you are doing a duologue, sit down with your partner and discuss your first impressions of the play and what it means to you. You are both going to need a very similar impression of the play for it to appear logical to the audience, examiner or audition panel. There will be a temptation to skim through the play and concentrate on 'getting on' with the text, as that is what will be seen, but it is worth remembering that often an examiner/audition panel will see what is not there as well as what is. A character who is out of context of the play will stand out straight away. Make sure you have understood the play as a whole before looking at your character in detail and starting work on your piece of text.

Acting tip

We do not act out a speech; we think and do as our character within a given situation. Do not think about how you are going to say the lines; instead, think about what your character wants and is doing.

78 THE FACTS OF THE PLAY

Student exercise

AIM

To list all the major facts you know about your character from the play.

- Work through the play, writing down all the facts you know about your character.
- Look for the following about your character:
  - age;
  - family details;
  - where your character grew up;
  - main childhood events;
  - main influence on your character from people, places and experiences;
  - education and employment; and
  - financial status.

Student follow-on exercise: context

- Fill in the gaps – all the information about your character that you could not find in the play.
- Use the context of the play and what you have already found out to help you work out the information you have not been given. For some plays, you might not be given much information, so you will need to logically create it through the next few exercises.

- For example, if the playwright does not tell you about your character's education, you will have to work backwards from what you do know. So, if my character is a doctor and lives in London, I would decide that I went to Med School at King's College, and at A level I studied Physics, Chemistry, Biology and Mathematics, getting A's in all four subjects. Then I would decide where I went to school and start to think about what interests I had.

79 RESEARCH

Student exercise

AIM

To find out about the period the play is set in.

- Research the period your play is set in.
- Find images and photos from that period to help you build a mental picture of your surroundings.
- Find photos that you can use for other family members and other characters in the play.
- Check on a map where your character was born and, if they moved, where they moved to.
- Start to decide on the social, economic, political and cultural influences of the time that would affect your character.
- Listen to the music and read one of the popular novels of the time to start to get pictures and impressions of the period the play is set in.

Notes for the student

The research stage is where you start to get all the information that can be channelled into creating your character. For example, if your character grew up during an economic depression, that would have an input into his or her development and would have an effect on how he or she viewed the world. Think of the research stage as your time to create pictures and images of the era your character lived in, his or her surroundings, friends, etc. so that when you come to create your character's past in the next exercise, you have all the data to help you.

80 MY CHARACTER'S PAST

Student exercise

AIM

To create your character's past.

- Using what you know from reading the play, analysing the facts and your research, create a past for your character.
- Find a quiet space and imagine your life from your first memory up until the moment that you first come on stage in the play.
- Write down the key events of your life as you have imagined them.
- If you are doing a duologue, sit opposite your partner and, if you are doing a monologue, sit opposite your teacher or a friend, and tell them your story. Remember to imagine the events as you describe them.
- Your partner or teacher can now ask you any questions on your character to make sure that you have created a rounded character with a full past.

Figure 5.1
Michaela is discussing the past of one of the characters she is preparing for her LAMDA gold medal

Student follow-on exercise: the park

- Go to your local park and imagine you are your character from a set day in your past.
- As your character, imagine you are sitting in your local park.
- What can you see?
- What can you hear?
- What would your character be thinking about?
- Now wander around the park and, as the character, imagine three different events from your life.

Student follow-on exercise: daily life

- Imagine a typical day in the life of your character.
- Imagine waking up, taking a shower, getting dressed, having breakfast. Think about what you do and where you go as your character.
- Remember to create pictures that fit in with the time your play is set and the country you live in.
- Gently imagine your daily life and how your routine makes you feel.

Notes for the student

You only need to imagine for a few minutes at a time. Do not try to force yourself to imagine for a long period of time. Gently imagining now and again is much better. This exercise will help you to start to freely build a character in a natural and relaxed setting. Creating a character is not just done in class or in the studio but 'up on your feet' as you go around your daily life. So, once you have done the park exercise, try the same thing in the car or eating lunch. By the time you come to share your character with your partner or teacher, you will already have a firm base on which to build your character's present and future.

So, for my character, the doctor from Exercise 78, I imagine going to the science museum as a child and being fascinated by everything I saw. Then, at 8 years old, I was coming home from school and there had been a car accident where a man walking past said that he was a doctor and started checking over the injured lady in the car. Watching this, my character thought, 'When I am older, I am going to be like him, be a doctor and help people'. By creating your past, you start to automatically create your future. An event in your character's past will have an effect on what your character wants in the present.

When you are imagining your character's past, refer to Exercise 1 in Chapter 1 on Stanislavski to help you. For a reference point, think about your life and the experiences you have had. You will need to produce pictures of your past with similar richness and detail.

81 MY FIRST MAIN MEMORY

Student exercise

> **AIM**
>
> To decide on your character's first main memory.

- Based on your experiences in the play and your character's past, decide on your character's first memory.
- Our first memories often have a big impact on our lives, so we need to create our character's first memory in order to understand him or her better.
- Tie in the memory with an event that happens in the play.
- Use your imagination to actively create this first memory with sense data so it feels like it actually happened.
- Put yourself in the situation of your first memory, imagining what you can see, hear, touch, taste and smell, and then imagine the events happening.
- Think about the thoughts that have come from your first memory and how, as the character, they have affected your life.

Notes for the student

Imagine you are rehearsing a monologue from *Macbeth* and you want to create your character's first memory. You can imagine that, at 6 years old, you were out with your father, the then Thane of Glamis, when you were temporarily separated because your father had seen a stag and went off in pursuit. While you were waiting, an old woman came up to you and told you that your father would be back soon but would have had an accident. The old woman disappears and then, when your father returns, you see that he has been thrown from his horse and is nursing a sore shoulder.

From that day, the incident plays in the back of your mind and you wonder how the old woman knew about your father. As you grow older, you hear of witches and decide she must have been one. Then, when you meet the witches at the start of the play, you have an in-built fascination for what they say. This main memory will help you to decide on the course of action you take.

In this way, you, as the actor, are connecting your character's past with his or her present, which will add a logical depth to your character. This enables you to build up a credible character based on active memories. When you meet the witches, the memory works as another input into what you are thinking and doing.

Acting tip

Do not get carried away and create memories that do not fit your character. If in doubt, run your memory past someone that has read the play and see if they agree that the memory fits the character.

82 MY CHARACTER'S FUTURE

Student exercise

AIM

To create your character's future.

You have created your past and now you need a future. The character on stage that we see during your monologue or duologue will have a purpose to his or her life; he or she will have aspirations and desires for the future. It is these aspirations that give your character a direction in his or her life and so it is these that we need to decide upon.

• Think about what your character wants out of his or her life.
• What do you think you, as your character, want to have achieved by the time you are 70?
• Give this impression (what you want) a label; for example, 'I want to be successful'.
• Now take a journey into the subconscious, as you did in Chapter 1 on Stanislavski, and decide on what you subconsciously want, and give that a label.
• This, then, is what you want and the direction you are going in.

Notes for the student

When I am watching students' monologues and duologues, I often ask them, 'What does your character want?' Often the response is a blank stare. We all want something in our lives and therefore we must want something as our character. It is your job to discover what it is your character wants so you know what path to follow. You can always fine tune what your character wants as you get further into the rehearsal process. This exercise will give your character purpose and direction on stage.

Figure 5.2
Reflecting on the
character's objective

83 MY PHYSICAL SELF

Student exercise

> **AIM**
>
> To create your character's physical self from your knowledge of his or her past and future.

- Find a space in the studio or a room at home and start to move around as your character, start to explore how you move and how you use the space around you.
- As your character, imagine you are waking up and brushing your teeth.
- As your character, pick an event from your past and walk it through as you imagine it happened.
- Relax and move around as your character, thinking about your past and what you want in the future. Allow this to feed into one distinct movement that sums up your character.
- While you are rehearsing, start to think about a movement that sums up all that your character is and wants.
- Allow yourself time to explore different movements until you have one movement that sums up your character and is the 'physical self' of your character.
- This movement will become your physical self and will act as a trigger to help you get into character.

Figure 5.3

Michaela exploring the physical self of Masha in Chekhov's *Three Sisters*

Notes for the student

Use your physical self to help you when rehearsing your character. Think of it as a 'way into' your character, almost like a hook that helps you hold on to all that you have created for your character. A few years ago, I was rehearsing a David Mamet play and, during a brief break, I was walking around the room as my character, muttering to myself. As I did this, a movement came to my character: I started to raise my arm up and down as if brushing someone off while, at the same time, the movement seemed to sum up my character's inner despair. I realised afterwards that this movement came from the character. I then used this movement to help me 'get into' character as I was rehearsing. It combined with what I was thinking and doing, and helped me create a rounded and detailed character.

This exercise is not about 'getting it right'. The movement will come from you as the character, so do not worry if nothing comes to you straight away. You will probably be sitting on the bus a week later thinking about your character and the movement will suddenly come to you.

84 MY CHARACTER'S GERM

Student exercise

AIM

To create your character's essence from your knowledge of his or her past and future.

- As you are walking to college or school or sitting on the train, think of one word that sums up your character.
- Like your physical self, which was one movement that sums up your character, this is one thought that sums up your character.
- Decide on one word that is the essence of your character. This will help you to understand who you are and what your character is like.
- So your character could think, 'I'm a loser' or 'I'm capable' or 'I'm lost'.
- Decide on your germ and, as you go through rehearsing your monologue or duologue, update it as you find out more about your character.

85 WHAT DO I THINK OF OTHER PEOPLE?

Student exercise

AIM

To create an impression of what you, as a character, think of the people around you.

- As your character, go back over your past and choose five key moments that involved other people.
- For each moment, imagine the circumstances and then decide what thoughts you had about the people involved in the key moment.
- Bring together all five key moments and jot down three thoughts you have about other people based on these past experiences.

- Keep these thoughts simple and remember to keep an impression of your character's past, future and germ while you are doing this exercise.

Student follow-on exercise: memory impro

- Choose one of the memories and, with one or two other students, improvise that memory.
- Try improvising a few different ways until you decide on one that best fits your character.
- Think about how improvising has helped you to create and, when you think about your character, evaluate how the memories that you improvised stick in your mind and seem to act as a reference point for your character.

Rehearsal tip

All these exercises can be done on your feet as you walk around Tesco or wait in the queue at Costa. Just bring in an impression of your character and think, 'What do I think of other people?' and the answer will pop up!

Notes for the student

This exercise will help you to decide what you think about other people and then how to behave with them. This exercise comes after the character's germ exercise, so you can build on what you think of yourself to combine this with what you think of other people. For example, my character may have the germ 'I'm selfish' and, when I was imagining a key moment, I imagined a time when, as a young boy, I was meant to be picked up after cricket practice by my elder sibling but they did not show up. Eventually, they arrived, saying they completely forgot about me. As a young boy, I thought, 'Well, people do not really care about me, so I am not going to care about them', which eventually becomes 'I'm selfish'.

Acting tip

A lot of your work as an actor is digging into your imagined past to come up with a logic for how you behave in the present. So keep digging and imagine away.

86 I AM BEING . . .

Student exercise

AIM

To start to create a totality for your character.

- Sit in a chair and start to imagine you are your character.
- Gently imagine your past and growing up.
- Bring in an impression of your germ and the thoughts that come from your germ.
- Imagine what your future will be like and your super objective.
- Gently think all these through and then imagine a circumstance from the play and put yourself in that circumstance.
- Imagine where you are and who is around you and what you think about them.
- Stand up and, as your character, get yourself a drink, pick up the newspaper or put a log on the fire. Walk about the room as your character and start to do the things your character would do.
- Allow yourself to gently think about all these things and see what you start to think and do within the circumstances.

Figure 5.4
Millie is imagining she is looking out of the window and reflecting on her situation as her character in Ostrovsky's *The Storm*

Notes for the student

This exercise is about you starting to gel together the different parts of your character. The best way to do it is as the character, experiencing the character's daily life. As you do this exercise, you will start to understand what your character is like, what he or she thinks and how he or she behaves. Just allow yourself to relax, gently imagine and start to think and do as the character.

Recently, I was working with a student preparing a monologue from *Uncle Vanya* for her LAMDA Gold. She had gone through all the exercises above but felt she still did not understand her character; she could not 'connect' with her character. I realised she was looking at her character from an academic perspective rather than putting herself in the position of the character. We did the 'I am being' exercise and everything seemed to fall into place for her; she sat in a chair and read a book while occasionally looking up to see if Astrov was paying any attention to her. I could see her start to think and do as Yeliena within the circumstance as she imagined her past, future and the actions she had with Astrov. She started to become active in the role and, after the exercise, looked at me and said, 'Ah, now I get what Yeliena's like'.

Notes for the teacher

A number of students who study drama often also choose literature as one of their options. So students may well come to you after having spent the last hour analysing Hamlet *from a very literary perspective, and you need to gently move them to analysing from the character's perspective. This exercise is perfect to accomplish this 'move' and helps give the student an active foundation on which to build their character.*

Rehearsal tip

There is only so much thinking *about* the character you can do; it is a good idea to start thinking *as* the character as early as you can in the rehearsal process.

87 BREAKING DOWN THE TEXT

Student exercise

AIM

To break up the text into manageable bits.

- Blow up your text on to an A3 piece of paper.
- Read over your text, looking for the changes in what your character is thinking and doing.
- Whenever there is a change, mark the change on your script.
- Number each change and give it a name.
- You should aim to end up with at least three changes over the course of your monologue or duologue.

Notes for the student

It is important to remember that you are rehearsing a short piece of text that will only last a few minutes, and that is what you will be assessed/judged on. In this exercise, you will break the text up to guarantee you can develop as a character and highlight your character's emotional journey. You are highlighting the changes in your text so you can create a structured piece that has a clear path and does not stagnate or go nowhere.

Students can often get stuck in 'doing the whole monologue the same'. By breaking up your text, you start to see where the changes will come and how they will affect your character.

Now you know where the changes in what your character is thinking and doing occur, you need to decide on what your character is thinking and doing, which will be covered in Exercises 88, 89 and 90.

88 WHAT ARE THE GIVEN CIRCUMSTANCES?

Student exercise

AIM

To decide on the character's given circumstances.

- Ask yourself:
  - Where am I?
  - What am I doing?
  - What has just happened?
  - What is the time?
  - Who is there with me, or am I alone?
  - What can I see?

Notes for the student

By asking yourself these questions, you start to put yourself in the given circumstances. You are creating the world around you that will lead on to what you are going to do as your character. Remember, it is always from the given circumstances that you, as the character, propel yourself into action.

Rehearsal tip

For some modern plays, there are very few given circumstances. In these cases, it is your job, as the actor, based on the logic of the character, to create them. In acting, we have to make decisions, and making a decision on the circumstances of the play is always better than not doing so.

89 WHAT DO I WANT?

Student exercise

AIM

To decide what you, as the character, want.

- For each change in the text, you need to give yourself an objective – what your character wants to achieve.
- Decide on your want and write it in the margin next to the bit of text it refers to, and then every time you are rehearsing your monologue or duologue, you can quickly remind yourself of your objective.
- Remember, to dig deep into what your character really wants, you need to delve into your character's subconscious and not just rely on what your character wants on the surface.
- Do not sit staring at the page in front of you, but get on your feet, put yourself in the circumstances and then ask, 'What do I want?' and see what answer your imagination comes up with.

Student follow-on exercise: the objective and the character

- At three different points during the day, imagine your given circumstances and then bring in your objective and see what happens to your character.
- Do this for about 15 seconds and then afterwards look back and see if the objective fitted your character. If it did not, think of another objective and try again.

90 WHAT IS MY ACTION?

Student exercise

AIM

To decide what you, as the character, are doing.

- Using the list of actions on page 31, decide on an action for the first bit of text before there is a change.
- Improvise the first bit with this action within the circumstances you have decided upon, and then go back and think about whether you had the action you decided on.
- Go through the other bits, giving each one an action, and then improvise.
- Remember, you can give an action to a word or line if you want to.
- Ask a fellow student to watch your piece, bit by bit, and see if they can spot what action you have, and ask them for feedback on whether they think you had the action and if it was the right one.

Student follow-on exercise: my through action

- Putting all the bits together, improvise your whole piece, concentrating on going from action to action.
- Improvise a few times until you start to think less about the actions as they become part of what you are doing subconsciously.
- As you do this, you will start to have an impression of a through action that takes you through the monologue or duologue.

Rehearsal tip

It often really helps to have someone watching you that can objectively guide you and offer feedback. But remember, in the end, you have to learn to have the ability to self-evaluate your own work.

91 RELATIONSHIPS

Student exercise

AIM

To decide on the relationships on and off stage.

- Write a list of the main characters you come into contact with during the course of the play.
- For each character, come up with one line that sums up your relationship with him or her.
- Try to dig deep into the subtext of the character to decide what you really think of him or her.
- If you are doing a duologue, you need to sit down with your partner and discuss your past relationship and what you think of each other.
- If, in your monologue, you talk about another character, make sure you think about your relationship with that person.

Notes for the student

When working out your relationships, try to dig deep into what your character really thinks. You may well think of someone as a good friend on the surface but underneath you might not trust him or her or are suspicious of his or her motives.

92 IMPROVISING TEXT

Student exercise

AIM

To improvise the piece, concentrating on thinking and doing as the character.

- Find a space, imagine your surroundings and improvise the 30 seconds leading up to the start of your monologue or duologue.

- Then continue with your piece, improvising a few times, thinking about what you want as your character, your action and keeping an impression of what you want in the future and your germ.
- After each time you have improvised the scene, pick up your text and check your lines and remind yourself of them, so each time you improvise you will get closer and closer to the actual text.
- Keep what you are thinking and doing as your character in mind at all times and do not worry about getting the words right.

Figure 5.5

Amy improvising as her character from the play

Notes for the student

Use this exercise to allow what your character is thinking and doing to settle. Allow your character to move around the space freely. If you, as the character, feel like sitting down or pacing, just do it. It is important to improvise the 30 seconds before the piece starts. This will help to establish your character in your mind and the audience's mind.

Rehearsal tip

Remember Exercise 83 on my physical self, and do not worry about where you are going to move. Allow the circumstances to guide you and allow your action to drive you around the stage.

93 OFF BOOK

Student exercise

> **AIM**
>
> To run the monologue or duologue.

- In a space, now run your monologue or duologue.
- Imagine your circumstances and first action and go for it.
- Do not think about what you should be doing as the actor; just allow the work you have done to take over.
- Run your piece a few times, allowing everything to settle. After each run, think back over your piece, checking for anything that might have dropped; for example, the germ or your character's past.

Notes for the student

This is the stage where, as the actor, you must 'let go' and experience your character. You have done all the work so now you must trust that it will be there and go for it.

94 OUTSIDE EYE

Student exercise

> **AIM**
>
> To get an observer's opinion.

- Show your piece to your teacher or a fellow student.
- Listen to their feedback and any recommendations they may have.
- If they do not understand your character or what your character is doing, think back over your preparation and see if you have missed anything out.

Figure 5.6
Watching Michaela perform her monologue before, as a group, we evaluated her performance

Notes for the student

This exercise helps you to find any holes in your performance. Often, someone can watch your piece and ask a simple question that you and your partner never thought about. If you feel yourself start to tense up as you are about to show your piece to someone, try to relax your body and mind as you learnt in Chapter 1 on Stanislavski.

Listen to the notes that your teacher and fellow students give you and then build them into the character you have created. For example, if you are directed to move across the stage at one particular point, do not just do it, but decide on why you are moving and the action that helps propel you to move.

95 COSTUME, PROPS AND MUSIC

Student exercise

AIM

To decide on costume, props and music to go with your piece.

- Chose costume and props that fit your character and the situation.
- Think about what would help to tell your story.
- Do not use props just to have something to hold, but think what your character would be holding at this point in the play.
- Decide on any music to be played before or during your piece.

96 THE FINAL RUN THROUGH

Student exercise

AIM

To add the final polish to your piece.

- Run your monologue or duologue at least a couple of times.
- Make sure you are comfortable with everything you are doing and do not change anything.
- The day of your exam or audition, do one last run through in the morning and then try to relax. If possible, this is the perfect time to take in a yoga class.

Student follow-on exercise: staying active

- At different points during the day before and the morning of your exam or audition, imagine yourself as your character as he or she goes about his or her daily life.
- So, as you are walking to the bus, imagine you are doing so as your character, and when you have lunch, have lunch as your character.

Notes for the student

You have done all the preparation, which leaves just the performance. Remember, you have done all the work, so really 'go for it', do not hold back, but allow yourself to fully experience your character. So, relax, go for it and, most of all, enjoy it!

6 Devising theatre

When devising a piece of theatre, the onus is very much on how you will work together in a group. It is about you exploring and creating together and coming up with something unique.

In many ways, there is no right or wrong way to devise. This chapter will take you through devising a piece step by step so you know you have the bases covered. In the previous chapters, you have a number of exercises to help you to create theatre; in this chapter, you will have a structure to plan your rehearsals. This chapter is to be used in conjunction with the chapters that have come before it. So far, you have amassed a series of exercises that can now be structured into devising theatre. This chapter is not intended to be prescriptive, so you can use a couple of the exercises here for structure and then, if you want to create a piece of political theatre, you can combine it with the exercises in Chapter 2 on Brecht.

When devising as a group, it is important to have an understanding of what you want to achieve and to decide on the direction of the piece. Often, pieces can come unstuck because the group does not have a clear focus on what they want to achieve. It is always a good idea to sit down as a group every couple of sessions and talk about whether you are still going in the direction you decided on. If you are not, then you can amend it so you all know that the direction has changed. Within this chapter, Exercises 112–116 will help you to create a piece of theatre in the style of Artaud. Artaud lived during the first half of the twentieth century and was a practitioner who created the 'theatre of cruelty', a style of theatre that aimed to break down the conformist plays of his time and to create a theatre that shocked the audience into questioning their own existence.

Ultimately, you will be creating a piece of new and original theatre. The best way to do that is by exploration, getting on your feet and trying different ways of doing things. If you have an idea, stand up, improvise it and see what happens. Then evaluate and see what worked and what did not work. Remember, some of what you do may never end up in your final piece, but you need to explore all the options as a way of creating your final piece.

I worked with a group of students who were devising and were about a month into rehearsing and had hit a bit of a brick wall. They had a basic structure but were missing something. One of the students went away and did some research and came back after having looked at how Meyerhold worked with his actors. The student had brought in five sticks and told the rest of the group that Meyerhold used sticks in some of his exercises so why do they not use sticks and see how it goes. The group then worked through some of Meyerhold's exercises using sticks. The piece ended up with each actor using the sticks to create the world of the play while also travelling from one scene to another. It highlighted the importance of research and how using the ideas of theatre practitioners can help spark off ideas. In the first four chapters of this book, you have exercises that will help you to trigger ideas and ways of doing things. So, if you hit a brick wall, go back a couple of chapters and see how Stanislavski, Brecht, Lecoq or Berkoff can help you out.

STARTING OFF

97 IDEAS, ISSUES AND THEMES

Student exercise

> **AIM**
>
> To decide on the key theme of your piece.

- As a group, sit in a circle, with any stimulus material in the centre.
- Give yourselves 20 minutes to discuss your central theme.
- Have one person jot down key ideas on a piece of card so you can track your discussions. Ideally, a large piece of card should be used so you can stick it up on the studio wall to refer to during rehearsals.
- Try to come up with a couple of key ideas that you can explore further.

Student follow-on exercise: the character's life

- On your way home, take one idea and decide on a setting and a character from that setting.
- Improvise a short 20 seconds in that character's life.

- Come into your group and show the 20 seconds.
- The rest of the group, watch and then join in as another character from the scene that has been created.

Notes for the student

Some of the best ideas come when you are not directly thinking about them. So, after you have sat down in your group, keep any ideas you have on the back burner and, every so often, think about the theme your group can use.

98 RESEARCH

Student exercise

AIM

To research your piece to start to trigger ideas.

- With your theme in mind, find out all you can about it.
- Find pictures of the time and look for novels and plays that are set at a similar period or deal with a similar issue.
- Think about where your piece will be set and the daily life of people who live during that period.
- Report back to your group with any images, diary entries, novels or real-life stories you have found and share them with your group.

Notes for the student

The research stage of any devised piece can be vital in helping you all to flesh out an idea. If you decide your theme is corruption, then go away and explore the theme from as many angles as you can. Do not worry how abstract a piece of research may be; this could always fuel your ideas as you go through the devising process.

99 USING A PRACTITIONER

Student exercise

AIM

To decide on which practitioner and style to use.

- Now you have an idea of your theme, think about which practitioner would work well to best explore your theme.
- In Table 6.1, a number of practitioners and styles are listed that you could choose from.

Table 6.1 Practitioner and styles

Stanislavski	comedy/tragedy
Meyerhold	melodrama
Knebel	farce
Brecht	commedia
Artaud	naturalism
Grotowski	realism
Lecoq	Epic theatre
Boal	political theatre
Brook	theatre of cruelty
Berkoff	creative adaptation
Mitchell	physical theatre

- Think about how you can incorporate the workings of your practitioner or style into your piece.
- Look back at Chapter 3 on Lecoq and Chapter 4 on Berkoff. The final sections of both these chapters give you a number of exercises that you can use to create a piece of theatre in the style of Lecoq or Berkoff.

Notes for the student

By choosing a style, you are choosing a practitioner, and vice versa. So, if you choose political theatre, you will end up using the ideas of Brecht. You will probably end up using more than one practitioner, so even if you decide to use Berkoff as your practitioner, it is still advisable to use some of the exercises you worked on in Chapter 1 on Stanislavski to help create your character. As a group, think about exploring and experimenting with your style so, from the outset, you give yourselves no boundaries and allow your imaginations to flow.

I remember watching one group devising a piece of theatre based on power. They were using the ideas of Boal and had done their research and came back with Boal's exercise 'the great game of power'. They put chairs in various positions around the space and then took the chairs away and took those places themselves. They used Boal's exercise as a springboard and then allowed it to develop and feed into their devising. It gave them the starting point for the scene and they ended up putting the chairs back in and using them in a slow motion piece set to coloured lights and eerie music. The overall effect was highly thought provoking, and showed what you can do when you experiment and give things a go!

Student follow-on exercise: plays and productions

- Look for plays that are in your selected style/practitioner and think about how you would bring the text to life.
- Go to see a production that relates to your chosen style or practitioner.

100 WHAT DO WE TELL THE AUDIENCE?

Student exercise

AIM

To decide on the purpose of the piece.

- As a group, start to think about what message you want the audience to get from your piece.
- Think about what you want them to leave the theatre thinking.
- Individually, write down one sentence that defines the message of your piece.
- Bring together all the sentences and, as a group, decide on one sentence that is your key message – what you want the audience to understand by your piece.
- Think about the subtext of your piece. What is its underlying message?

Student follow-on exercise: political, social and cultural message

- Decide whether or not your piece has a political message.
- What do you want to tell the audience about society today or when the play was set?
- How has the culture of the time of your piece affected society and mankind?
- How can you weave these issues into your piece, whether on a conscious level or a more subconscious level?

Notes for the student

By deciding on the key message of your piece, you will, as a group, give your piece a direction. It is quite easy when devising to start to create a series of scenes and characters without having decided where you really want to end up. So, if your theme is corruption, you may end up deciding that your message is 'the rich get richer, the poor get poorer'. Then, as you go through the process of devising your piece, you always have a clear purpose to what you are doing on stage. This then not only helps you to shape your performance, but helps the audience to understand it too. When thinking about the subtext of the piece, decide what you are really telling the audience. So, for the theme of corruption, on the surface the message may be that society and its institutions are corrupt, but underneath through drama you are asking questions about human nature and whether we are, as individuals, inherently corruptible.

101 EXPLORING IDEAS

Student exercise

AIM

To explore and develop your group's ideas or central theme.

- Take your first idea and, as a group, stand in a circle.
- Using all the ideas you have researched, decide on a setting and character.
- One by one, step into the circle as a character and tell your story.
- Try to keep your story in line with your decided theme.
- Tell your story as the character in around 30 seconds.
- After you have all told your story, examine the characters you have created and start to think about how they could all fit together.

Figure 6.1
Students discussing ideas
for devising their scene

Student follow-on exercise: in the circle

- Now go around the circle again as your character and, as you walk into the circle, one person from the group shouts out a new setting and someone else from the circle joins the person in the middle of the new setting.
- Try this a few times, building quick scenes between your characters as you go.

Notes for the student

As you do this exercise, think about the message of your piece, keeping in mind your practitioner and style, and see what happens. In the early stages of devising, you may well only get a few seconds of material that you eventually use, but you will often trigger an idea or an interesting path to follow.

102 PLOT THROUGH LINE

Student exercise

AIM

To mark out the main stages of your piece.

- Write down the ten main events or stages of your piece.
- Think about the main plot line and any sub-plots you want to have running at the same time.
- Use this as an outline for the next few rehearsals.

Student follow-on exercise: in a minute

- As a group, improvise your piece in 1 minute.
- Use the plot outline, bearing in mind your message and the first thoughts you have on characters.
- Talk about it for about 5 minutes then get up on your feet and see where the piece goes.
- Afterwards, evaluate and discuss what you have discovered.

Notes for the student

This exercise should give you a clear grasp of where you are going with the piece and will give you confidence in the skeleton of the piece that you have stood up and performed. Try to do this exercise within the first couple of weeks of starting your devising project so you do not spend too long sitting and talking. Get on your feet and start exploring.

Remember, what you decide here is not where you will end up, but it will give you an outline on which to build and grow your piece.

103 CREATING A CHARACTER

Student exercise

AIM

To create an impression of your character.

- Decide on who your main character is and then, using the exercises in Chapter 1 on Stanislavski, start to create a character.
- Do the work on your feet as you go around school, college or university.
- Imagine a circumstance your character would be in and improvise 20 seconds as the character.
- Go into your group and show your character and, as a group, discuss how this character fits with the designed plot and message of the piece.

Notes for the student

You may well be playing a number of roles, sharing the main role between the group or working within an ensemble. If this is the case, it is always a good idea to think about your character or role and what they want to achieve in the piece. Even if your role is part of an ensemble, you still need to know what you want and what you are doing. I recently watched an ensemble piece with the chorus on stage throughout the piece taking it in turns to play the main role. The piece was littered with exciting physical choral work that was very impressive. Unfortunately, in between these impressive moments, the chorus switched off and waited for 'their next bit'. Sometimes, there is nothing worse than watching an actor stand on stage with no character, waiting for his 'next bit'.

Student follow-on exercise: setting

- As a group, decide on where you will set your piece.
- Be creative while thinking what location or locations would symbolically help the audience to understand your piece.

104 DEEPENING YOUR CHARACTER

Student exercise

AIM

To explore the physical depths of your character.

- Walk around the space as your character.
- Think about the theme of your piece and your main character.
- As you walk, start to put your character in different circumstances and see how you react physically.
- Allow a movement or gesture to come from your character that seems to express what your character is thinking and feeling.
- Move around using this gesture within your character's daily life.
- Keeping your gesture in mind throughout the devising process, use it as a way to connect with your character.

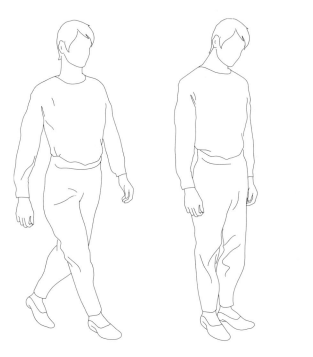

Figures 6.2a–c
Deepening your character

Figure 6.3
Amy reflecting on her
character's inner journey

Notes for the student

Sometimes, when devising, it helps to have a movement or gesture that can act as the key to your character both internally and externally. Keep this key in mind to help with the highs and lows of your character.

Rehearsal tip

Regardless of which practitioner and style you are working on, you will always need to create a character. If you are a devising for GCSE, A level, IB or BTEC, check the specifications to see if marks are awarded for creating and developing a role.

WORKING ON INDIVIDUAL SCENES

105 GETTING UP ON YOUR FEET

Student exercise

AIM

To devise the opening of your piece.

- Decide on the setting and what has just happened, and then improvise the opening of your piece.
- Improvise it a couple of times, building on the work each time.
- Using actions from Chapter 1 on Stanislavski, plot how your actions change over the piece and write them down.
- Discuss what you have improvised and brainstorm any ideas to add to the opening, then improvise again.

Notes for the student

It is always a good idea to use actions (see Chapter 1 on Stanislavski) to help you to decide what your character is doing. If you devise your opening, then at a later stage you can add a symbolic opener to your piece that represents the piece as a whole. Then you can start with an ensemble physical opening to establish the piece and move into your opening scene that will support the narrative.

Figure 6.4

Starting a scene

Rehearsal tip

Have an A3 sheet of paper for each scene and mark on the paper the results of your improvisations and devising, keep this as a journal to record the devising process.

106 A LETTER

Student exercise

AIM

To start building your piece in role.

- Stand in a circle, with a piece of paper in an envelope in the centre of the circle.
- In turns, go into the centre of the circle and, as one of your characters, open the letter and react to what you read.
- Think about how you can react physically and verbally to what is written.
- Try not to decide beforehand what is in the letter; rather, in role, allow yourself to be spontaneous.

Student follow-on exercise: adding setting

- This time, go around the circle but decide on the setting your character is in before you walk into the circle.
- While you are watching the person in the middle, if you have an idea, get up on your feet and join them in the middle.

Notes for the student

When you read the letter, imagine what you are reading is related to your character or an event of the play. Use this as a springboard for ideas on how your character would react and then build on them. If a moment or a sequence works well, think about integrating this into your piece.

107 WITH STICKS

Student exercise

AIM

To start to use props creatively.

- As a group, hold a stick (bamboo or broom handles are best) and stand in a triangular shape, leaving enough room between you to swing your stick.

Figure 6.5
With sticks

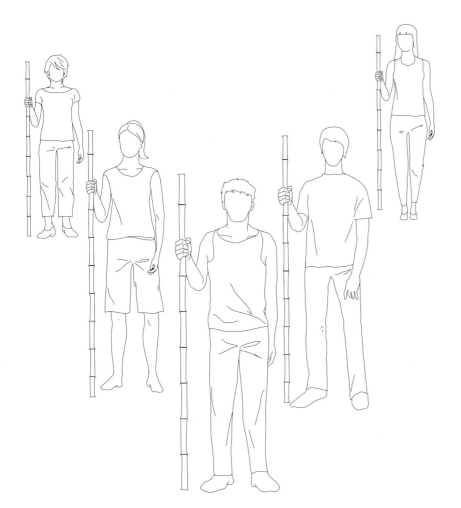

- With the person at the front of the triangle acting as the leader, mirror how they are standing and holding their stick.
- The leader starts to move their stick in hand slowly, with the rest of the group following.

Figure 6.6
With sticks 2

- Start to build a rhythm as a group working as an ensemble.
- Slowly start to move around the room, working in time and keeping the same shape.
- Run this several times until you are all working together in time.
- Now add a purpose to the movement (why you are doing it) that links to your piece and the message of your piece.
- Think how you can use the sticks to show how you feel as a group within the piece.

Student follow-on exercise: create your world

- Think how you can use the sticks to create the space you are working in.
- Try using them to link scenes or to create a recurring image throughout the piece.

Notes for the student

This does not mean that you have to use sticks within your devised piece. It might be that it would not fit with the style you have chosen. This exercise is to help you to try different approaches and to experiment with what works and what does not.

108 PASS THE BALL

Student exercise

> **AIM**
>
> To find the rhythm and pace of your piece.

- Take a scene and stand in the position you would start the scene in.
- The first person to speak starts with a ball.
- On the line, throw the ball to the person you are saying that line to. That person then catches the ball and throws it to the person they speak to next on the line of dialogue.
- Throw the ball around as a group, and use the ball to reflect the rhythm of the scene and also to guide it.
- Allow the energy of what you are doing and saying to be reflected in the throwing of the ball.

Student follow-on exercise: using pace

- Run the scene again, this time throwing the ball in time, so not on the line but in time and rhythm.
- Now try a completely different rhythm – one that is disjointed and uneven – and see how that affects the scene.

Notes for the student

Play around with the pace and rhythm of the scene using the ball and see what effect it has on the scene when you take the ball away. This can be very useful when you have a dialogue-heavy scene that seems to be dragging and you need to give it a boost of energy.

109 FREEZE A SCENE

Student exercise

AIM

To help with a tricky scene.

- Take a scene that you are unsure about and, as a group, create five or six tableaux that highlight the main events of the scene.
- Take those tableaux and think how you can add sound then movement.
- Think how you can symbolise what your piece is about in this scene through your use of the space.
- Try doing the series of tableaux to music with movement to link each tableau, taking out the dialogue and allowing your movement and actions to speak for you.

Notes for the student

It is quite normal to hit a wall during the devising process. As a group, you have got to the stage where Annie and I often go into schools and colleges to run our workshops. It is often an injection of ideas that can give you a different way of looking at your piece and help you to move forward.

I often find this exercise, where you go back to tableaux and then build movement and voice with music, can create an active and vibrant scene. I also work on actions so everyone is clear on what they are doing and what they want, so the scene has a real totality. I remember a workshop Annie gave where she took an A2 group and took them through Exercise 55 on climbing the fence. The group had got very bogged down in heavy dialogue, and this exercise helped them to think differently and to express themselves physically within the context of their piece.

Rehearsal tip

Often, devising a piece can cause tension within a group. Refer back to Exercise 3 on free body relaxation and regularly run a relaxation exercise at the start of your rehearsals.

110 SCENE CHANGES

Student exercise

AIM

To design fluid and interesting scene changes.

* Think about how you will move from one scene to the next.
* Create a sequence that can be used to flow between scenes.
* Think how this sequence can represent the message of the piece as it recurs.

Devising tip

Keep a record of everything you devise as you go along. You can have a log book to record each scene or film each bit you devise so you can go back over it and see what you have created.

Notes for the student

If this is done effectively, the scene changes can become an integral part of the piece. Years ago, I saw a version of Lorca's *Blood Wedding* in Moscow. The scene changes were choreographed movement pieces that built in tension and ferocity as the play evolved. The whole cast acted as an ensemble and afterwards it was hard to imagine how the play would have worked without the ensemble sequences. Try out a few different ways of moving from one scene to the next, thinking of how you can use pace to reflect the narrative of your piece.

111 UNIQUE STAGING

Student exercise

AIM

To create a piece of unique staging.

- Halfway through the rehearsal period, sit together in your group and start to discuss ideas for a piece of unique staging.
- You may well be able to use ideas already discovered so far or you may want to create an entirely new scene.
- This scene will be unique and a chance to show off your creativity.
- Think about how, using movement, space and sound, you can symbolise the very essence of your piece.
- Use choral work from Exercise 67 on the base pulse and Exercise 68 on the Greek chorus, and the next few exercises on Artaud.
- Decide on how lighting and music can support your stage work.

Figure 6.7
Students working on a piece of unique staging when devising. You can tell this is the first time they have tried it by the smiles on their faces

Rehearsal tip

Do not hold back on your ideas; if someone has an idea, explore it and see where it takes you.

Notes for the student

This is your chance to come up with something special! If your piece is being externally examined, it is your chance to make the examiner sit up and see you create something unique. You can start simple and build up as you go along, adding the different exercises you have explored through this book. Try to think 'outside the box' and see where you end up.

USING ARTAUD

112 THE ARTAUD EFFECT

Student exercise

AIM

To help create an Artaudian effect within your piece.

- For your piece, think about how you can alter the staging and use of space to challenge the audience and question their perceptions of your piece.
- Work on using alternative lighting states that will help to communicate directly with the audience. Try lighting states that are in stark contrast to the action of a given scene.
- Work on your vocal projection and how you are using your voice to threaten and challenge the audience.
- Think about how to represent your views on mankind and the society we live in.
- Think about breaking down the conventions of typical theatre; change the space, staging, use levels and movement all to create a different and spiritual experience.
- Contrast the emotions used with the action of the play to create an unnerving effect for the audience.
- Create a specific rhythm and tempo to your piece and use it to link and develop the scenes within your piece.
- Work into your piece the relationship between dreams and reality and how they affect our journeys through life.

Notes for the student

Artaud wrote about what he thought theatre should be like but, unlike Stanislavski, Brecht, Lecoq and Berkoff, he did not leave behind a way of working that can be used by actors to create the kind of theatre he wanted. If you are using Artaud, you can use a number of the exercises in this chapter combined with those in Chapter 2 on Brecht and Chapter 4 on Berkoff to give your piece the Artaudian effect. When we talk about 'threatening the audience', Artaud was more interested in creating a theatre that challenged and broke with tradition, a theatre that took the audience on a spiritual journey of discovery about the natural world around us. Artaud wanted you, as actors, to harness the power of your body, voice, mind and spirit combined with the power of the sounds and sights of the world around us to create theatre; a theatre that is very personal and should come from the performer and the natural world combined. If you have chosen Artaud as your practitioner or style, the next three exercises will help you to create your Artaudian theatre.

113 HARNESSING NATURE

Student exercise

AIM

To use and harness the physical world around us.

- Imagine, as a group, you are standing in a gale.
- Imagine the gale buffeting your bodies, and start to move in time with the gale as it crashes through the space.
- The gale changes direction and you have to adapt to the change.
- Now stand still and imagine the gale has died and there is just a gentle breeze blowing on to you.
- In your group, using movement and your breath to support your movement, move from the breeze back to the gale.
- Work in time with each other, reacting to the wind and each other so you start to all work in harmony.
- Now, as a group, follow the same process with fire, building towards working as a group going from the feeling of a raging forest fire to the flame of a candle.
- Within your piece, create a movement sequence that reacts and responds to the physical elements as you did in this exercise.
- Think about using the energy from this exercise and filtering it into your piece.

114 SOUNDSCAPE

Student exercise

AIM

To add sound to the opening scene.

- Using the scene you have improvised, keeping the actions of your character in mind, go through the scene using percussion instruments to replace the dialogue.
- Run the scene using the instruments to create a rhythm in the scene.
- Aim to create a soundscape that reflects the subtext of the scene.
- Then, once you have a clear rhythm, add the dialogue back to the scene in harmony with the soundscape.

Student follow-on exercise: movement scape

- Now run the scene but without sound and speech. Use movement to replace the sounds from the previous exercise.
- Your movements can be abstract, and you can start to work together as an ensemble within the piece.
- Keep in mind your actions and allow them to drive the movement within the scene.

Notes for the student

This exercise can create some fascinating movement that organically has come from the improvisations. If you end up moving as an ensemble or all freezing at a given point, then mark these down as you go along so you can build on it when you come to work on this scene again. Always keep in mind how you are using the space and the message this communicates to the audience.

115 CHORAL REPETITION

Student exercise

> **AIM**
>
> To explore working as an ensemble chorus.

- Take a short piece of dialogue from a scene or a poem or lyrics from a song that fit with your piece.
- Stand with one person in front of the group. The person at the front then says the first line.
- The next two people behind the front person repeat the line, varying the volume and texture of the words.
- The next two people repeat the line again but in an opposite way to the two before them.
- Then all repeat the line again as a group, as an ensemble.
- Move on to the next line, working from the back to the front, with the rest of the group echoing the line.
- Once you have a chorus of a few lines, use the same process to add movement and use pace to build to a climax.

Student follow-on exercise: contrast

- Try breaking the text up so different people have different lines from the poem and, as you move together as one, you use your voices in contrast to the movement.
- You can then vary the movement while keeping the vocal part in time.

Notes for the student

This kind of exercise can allow you, as a group, to play with voice and working as a chorus. It will help you to transform a scene and help to build in tension and climax to your piece. I recently worked with a group who took the lines from William Blake's *The Tiger* and, in a large extended triangle covering the whole space, started in a whisper repeating the chorus as they moved and froze, moved and froze. The sequence built up to a powerful crescendo, exploding into an ensemble scream. As the lights went down, a solitary figure whispered the first two lines of the poem and the group moved eerily on to the next scene.

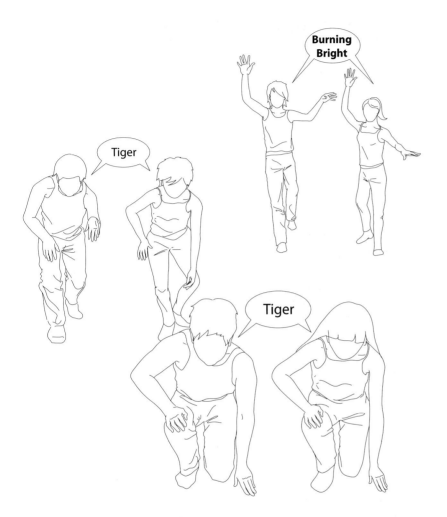

Figure 6.8
Choral repetition

Notes for the student

I was working with a group looking at the theme of war and how it destroys lives. The central character did this exercise and used the physical action of cleaning her rifle as the action. She then broke this down into four movements expressing how she felt being in a war zone. The rest of the group were all stationed around the stage on different levels, mirroring her sequence. They all started slowly, building up each time they repeated the four movements in time. As they went, they added text – 'pain', 'fear', 'mother', 'daughter' – and used their voices and musical instruments to heighten the tension as they went. The scene became quite harrowing; the group played footage of a child victim during the Vietnam War on a loop during the scene and used extracts from John Cage's *A Flower* to give the scene a very harrowing and ultimately Artaudian effect.

Figure 6.9
Using Artaud as their practitioner, the students started to experiment with theatre that made the audience feel uncomfortable

Figure 6.10
The girls use the camera lens as their eye line, imagining this to be their audience. I think Matt, the photographer, was quite taken aback

BRINGING EVERYTHING TOGETHER

116 MUSIC, COSTUME AND PROPS

Student exercise

AIM

To decide on costume, props and music to go with your piece.

- Think about music that you could use with your piece. Try not to pick songs that you like, but rather ones that help communicate the message of your piece while supporting the narrative.
- Keep in mind your style and practitioner when you choose the music.
- With costume choices, you may want to symbolise what your character is like internally or make a statement about society or class.
- Think about if you are going to use props or not.

Student follow-on exercise: props or no props

- Run a scene that you are using props in and then run the same scene without props.
- Speed up the scene and then slow down the scene without props and see what the effect is on the scene.

Notes for the student

Try not to leave costume, props and music to the last minute. Think about them as you go along and start to integrate your costume choices into rehearsals. Music can have a real impact on the audience and, combined with characters in role in the space, can really affect the mood of the audience. I recently watched a devised piece where, towards the end following the death of the leading character, the space went dark. As a spotlight came up on one of the cast playing the violin, the others moved as an ensemble, representing the loss of the person that had died. The overall effect was highly charged and left the audience emotionally reeling. It reminded me how simple movement and music can have a dramatic effect.

117 PREPARING THE SPACE

Student exercise

AIM

To create a space to work in.

- Think about the space you are going to present your devised piece in.
- Look around at what you have in the performance space and think how you can use it.
- Decide how you can create levels and use a set that will help with the message of your piece.
- Do you have a corridor next to the studio that can be used? Is there a balcony that you have access to?

Notes for the student

On a recent visit to a school, I saw students rehearsing their devised piece up a tree in the school grounds. They had created a tree house and were staging their piece on ground level, with some action above them in the tree house. I watched for a while and smiled; the students had 'thought outside the box' and looked to be having the time of their lives!

118 RUNNING THE PIECE

Student exercise

AIM

To run the piece in the allocated time.

- You will have a series of scenes that now needs running.
- Set a stopwatch for the allocated time, clear the space, pre-set all costume and props and then run your piece.
- For the first run, try not to stop but go through all the scenes you have designed so you get a feel for the piece as a whole.
- Run the piece several times to start to understand the rhythm of the piece as a group.

Notes for the student

Running your devised work is always an essential part of the process. You need to run it enough times for you all to feel comfortable within the piece while, at the same time, not over running it so you start to lose the active impulses of the characters.

119 WATCHING FROM THE OUTSIDE

Student exercise

AIM

To get an observer's opinion.

- Show your piece to your teacher or a fellow student.
- Listen to his or her feedback and any recommendations he or she may have.
- If he or she does not understand your piece or what your piece is about, then, as a group, think how you can make your message clearer.

Notes for the student

I will often watch a devised piece and then afterwards ask the students a simple question about the structure of the piece, and I will see on their faces that it is something that has never crossed their minds. Often, it is only when someone outside the group watches your piece that things will get picked up on. You can then, as a group, use this feedback to improve your piece.

Student follow-on exercise: walking your role

- At home, find a quiet space and walk through your role in the piece.
- Start with arriving at the studio and setting up, then start to bring in your character and walk through everything that happens in your piece.
- Do not rush, but imagine the space you would be in and where you have to go, what you have to do and what you need to think.
- Use this time to walk slowly what you are to do during the performance.

Notes for the student

This follow-on exercise really helps you to get in the right frame of mind to run your piece. The devising process can be quite a frantic experience, and this gives you time to walk through every second on stage. After having done this, you will feel like you are ready and will be safe in the knowledge that you know exactly what you should be doing.

120 THE FINAL RUN

Student exercise

AIM

To add the final polish to your piece.

- Schedule a run in front of an audience a couple of days before your first night or showing to an examiner.
- After the dress, meet as a group and discuss how you felt it all went.
- Use this run to help cement your role within the piece.

Notes for the student

The first time you run a piece before an audience, your mind is often racing and you feel as if you do not have enough time to do all you have to do on stage. After a week of shows, you feel like you have all the time in the world and cannot really remember what it was like on the first night. This is the process that all performers go through, and a piece can never be ready until it is performed to an audience. This performance helps to set the piece and gel everything together in a way that cannot be done through running a piece without an audience.

It is quite common for things to change a bit on the first couple of runs, with some things being missed or added in. This too is part of the first days of running a piece, so if something happens that did not happen before just relax and improvise. The chances are you will be back on track before you know it and the audience will not have noticed a thing.

We all suffer from nerves, some more than others, so in the half hour before the show find a space and run a relaxation exercise. Allow this to focus you on what you have to do next and then, depending on the demands of your piece, you can go into a vocal and physical warm-up.

7 Improvising with a practitioner

This chapter will give you the opportunity to practise the ideas that you have encountered in this book. Each exercise in this chapter is a different scenario for you to work at on your own, then in pairs and finally in a group.

First, read the improvisation, then pick a practitioner to use and then improvise in the style of that practitioner. Think about how that practitioner worked and what you would need to incorporate within the improvisation to achieve the style of your chosen practitioner.

So, if for Exercise 123 I choose Berkoff, then I think about what I have learnt and experienced in Chapter 4 on Berkoff to help me create a piece of total theatre. Alternatively, I may choose Brecht and then think of all the techniques I can use to create a piece of epic theatre.

This chapter is about you freely exploring the different practitioners and styles. You can start to use the different practitioners together, so you use Stanislavski to create a character, Brecht to define the message of your performance and Lecoq to create some truly symbolic and imaginative staging within your improvisation. You can improvise these spontaneously or you can plan them in greater detail and then improvise based on the planning you have done.

121 ON THE EDGE

Student exercise: one-person improvisation

*   You are on a gap year after finishing your studies and before you go to university. You live in Chicago and your boyfriend is a keen climber. You have decided to go climbing together and, as you are a novice, you have started with quite an easy slope. You have been practising on the climbing wall at school for the last 6 months but you are still a bit scared of heights and, every so often, you have to stop and try to control your breathing.

Your boyfriend Brad has climbed on ahead and you hear a scream from him. You are not sure what has happened but can see his foot on a ledge a few feet up from you.

You have called out his name and he is not answering, so you decide to steady yourself and climb the few feet up to him.

- The improvisation will start with you checking your equipment and rope and then going for Brad.

Notes for the student

For this improvisation, you may well use a combination of practitioners to create the physicality and the tension that your character would be feeling.

122 THE HOT CHEF

Student exercise: one-person improvisation

- You are a chef; you adore food and its creation more than anything else. Tonight, you have invited your old high school sweetheart over for dinner. Your party piece is cooking in front of your guest while you talk them through what you are doing, how you are going to cook the food and the origin of the dish.
- The time is now 8.15, the ingredients you will prepare are laid out in front of you; sitting on a stool in front of you is Rebecca, sipping a glass of champagne and watching you eagerly. You smile, pick up your knife and explode into a passionate discourse on what you are preparing.
- You use flamboyant and extravagant language, pronouncing every syllable in your keenness to depict the true culinary delight that the lovely Rebecca will soon be feasting on.

123 STRIKE ACTION

Student exercise: paired improvisation

- Your name is Kate and you work in a primary school. You are now 34 and have been teaching for 10 years. Recently, the government made changes to teacher pensions and you will now have to work a bit longer and will have to pay more for your pension. You are okay with this, as a number of your old school friends have private pension plans that are not half as good as yours, so you think on reflection you are quite well off.

A strike has been called by your union for next week over the government's pension plan. In passing, you told the union official that you would be working next Thursday and not striking. He looked shocked and started to argue with you about the issue. Not wanting to get into a row, you smiled and said you had to teach and walked off. He has seen you twice already about the issue and will not let it go.

- Tony, you are a teacher at Kate's school and a union official for the biggest school union. You see it as your job to motivate the staff to fight the government. When you first heard that pensions were to be changed, you were disgusted, and see this as another example of the ruling classes oppressing the worker. Most of the staff are supporting the strike; even the head teacher is going to man the picket line. Only two teachers are not striking: Francis, the six-foot-three PE specialist, and Kate. When you spoke to Francis, he laughed as he was not willing to lose a day's pay but would strike if you covered his wages. You find Francis quite intimidating so you left it at that.

  Kate, however, is quite quiet and you are sure you can push her into striking; you cannot stand people that do not stand up for their rights. Walking past her room, you see through the window that she is marking and decide this is the perfect time to get her on side.

- It is now 3.45. Kate, you are marking some work and Tony the union official comes in brandishing the latest report on how much more pension you will have to pay. You have had enough, and think it is time to explain to Tony about an individual's freedom of choice.

Student follow-on exercise: with a practitioner

- Decide on your practitioner and improvise the scene, then, in your pair, evaluate how using the practitioner may have helped the improvisation. Once you have improvised with one practitioner, swap roles and choose a different practitioner and see if you get a different result.

124 'SPOONS'

Student exercise: paired improvisation

- You are 'Spoons' Smith. You are 42 and a gangster from the East End of London. Your manor is Bethnal Green; everyone in Bethnal Green belongs to you, you own the streets. You got the nickname 'Spoons' after you took down the legendary Conway brothers with just a spoon. You are now standing in front of your second in command, 'Scrubs' Henderson. One of your guys came to you this afternoon with news that 'Scrubs' was rumoured to be part of a job set up for tomorrow night on the borders of your manor and that he has been working with a rival gang. In your hand you hold a spoon.

- You are Scrubs. You have worked for Spoons for over 5 years and have always been loyal.

  A week ago, you were out in a club when a girl was talking to you about a deal going down that could earn serious money. You had had a few drinks and it all sounded like a good idea at the time. You gave the girl your card and then forgot all about it until a couple of days ago when she shows up at your car lot and says that tonight is the night for the job, and, as agreed, she needs two 'clean' cars and for them to disappear afterwards. You start to panic and tell her you cannot get involved because it is on Spoons' manor. She hands you the address for the drop off point for the cars, turns and laughs as she is walking away.

- The improvisation will start with Spoons walking around Scrubs describing exactly what he is going to do to him and how he will make his last day on earth a painful one – unless, of course, he tells him everything and swears complete loyalty.

Figure 7.1
Improvising a scene

125 FALLOUT

Student exercise: four-person improvisation

- The year is 2063. In the year of 2041, a small nuclear device was detonated by a terrorist group in downtown Manhattan. The government of the US responded with a strike on military targets belonging to the government of North Korea. The government of North Korea launched an all-out attack on the US and her allies and, within 24 hours, the world as it was known no longer existed.

- You are a group of four 22 year olds. When the war started, you were all newborns in a hospital in New York. The hospital had a bunker installed during the cold war that was still fully operational. As the first missiles were launched, a nurse took you all to the bunker. You were brought up together in the bunker and that is where you spent the first 5 years of your lives.

- When you were all 5, the nurse who had saved you took you to her old family home just outside Southampton where you have grown up. Only on two occasions have you encountered other survivors who were journeying to find a community to live in. Two weeks ago, a lone traveller told you about a community of over 200 people that exists near Atlantic City. Tonight, over dinner, you all discuss what the traveller had said. Jake and Lucy, you want to go and find the community, whereas Ellen and Naomi want to stay where you are, fearful of what you could find. A few years ago, around the time the old nurse passed away, Jake had seen what looked like the mutated form of a man scavenging. None of you know what is really out there and you feel safe out on Long Island.

- The world you live in is very different from the one the nurse used to tell you about. Life is slowly restoring itself, but the process will take generations. The permanent grey that shrouded the planet in the years after the war has lifted, but the temperature is still rarely above freezing.

- The improvisation starts with Jake saying he wants to go in search of the community.

126 ART

Student exercise: four-person improvisation

- You belong to a local art appreciation group. You meet every week at Nigel's house and discuss a different painting. Nigel, your group leader, has arranged for you to view a new exhibition by a young artist, Tarquin.
- Nigel, you are 42, single and live alone. You studied History of Art at university and have chaired the art appreciation group for the last 3 years. You met Tarquin recently at a gallery opening and were extremely interested in his vision of modern art. You accepted his invitation to bring your group to the opening of his exhibition. You love classic art and particularly the Renaissance period. As you are walking along the street on your way to the gallery, you realise that Tarquin was very vague about his actual work, always talking in terms of light and colour and not content.
- Penelope, you are 26 and a recent graduate from art school. You met Nigel a few months ago and have been coming to his sessions for a few months and love the chance to meet like-minded art lovers. Also, as Dallas is a member of the group and a famed art critic, you hope he will come to your first exhibition when it opens later in the year. You asked a friend if they had heard of Tarquin, as you were going to his exhibition, and they laughed and wished you luck. As you walk towards meeting the others, you wonder if Nigel knows what he is letting you all in for.
- Lesley, you are 35 and teach art at a local secondary school. You are always keen to see what is going on in the art world so you can steal ideas for your A level students' coursework pieces. Often, you feel a bit out of your depth when you hear Dallas and Nigel talk, and you often disagree with them just to make it seem as if you have a real opinion when often you are not really sure.
- Dallas, you are 52 and have worked as an art critic for over 20 years and are famous for having made a number of today's top artists, and at the same time destroying the careers of others. When you see art, you go off your gut instinct and have no qualms about telling an artist exactly what you think.
- Tarquin, this is your second exhibition. Your first, in New York, was closed after only 2 days because of complaints. It featured a number of religious leaders superimposed into the context of the work on a different religion. As your exhibition was closed, you cursed the morality police and decided to stage your next exhibition in London.
- The improvisation will start with Nigel, Penelope, Lesley and Dallas meeting at Holborn tube station and walking a few doors down to the

gallery. As you walk in, you are greeted by Tarquin, dressed in a pair of swimming trunks. He greets you all warmly and shows you through to the exhibition. The walls are lined with Tarquin in various stages of undress at key European landmarks. At the end of the room is a large painting of a mountain with a photo of Tarquin on the top. Nigel, you are instantly embarrassed and wish you had questioned Tarquin more about his 'paintings'. Lesley, you are altogether undecided if this is art or not. Dallas, you cannot believe this guy is for real. Penelope, you are looking at the floppy-haired Tarquin in his schoolboy swimming trunks and have decided you really do quite like this chap.

127 ON THE COUCH

Student exercise: five-person improvisation

- Tiago, you are a psychiatrist. You were born in Portugal and now practise psychiatry in Leeds. You have pioneered a new way of dealing with the problems of the mind through physical expressionism. This involves getting your patients to physically express their problems through the medium of movement and mime. Today, you have a group of three patients that meet with you every Wednesday and have done for 2 months now. You believe in group counselling to 'share and triumph' together. Today, the patients are going to be doing 'the animal'. They choose a key moment in their lives that has affected them, one that they have not already shared and triumphed, and decide on an animal that best expresses the memory they feel. They then move into the space and create the animal. An abstract delivery is fine as long as they use the moment in their lives to guide them.

- Debbie, you are an English teacher from Wrexham. You work in a secondary school just outside the M25. Before becoming a teacher, you were a model and, as you have got older, you have grown more and more depressed. It used to be you would walk into a bar and the bar would stop and all eyes would be on you, but now, as you battle your way through your late 40s, it is rare for you even to get a compliment. You came to Tiago after 2 years of depression and frustrated outbursts. You are naturally outgoing and while you are with the group you can almost forget your age and be the girl you once used to be.

- Hugh, you have just turned 40 and work for the NHS. After university, you went to Sandhurst and joined the army. You left after 8 years at the rank of Captain. Now, looking back, those were the best days of your life; skiing trips, exercises in far-flung places and living in Germany with the liveliest officers' mess in NATO. Towards the end of your career, you were posted to Bosnia for a 6-month tour. One July day, you saw something while on patrol that has never left your mind. Even now as you sit at your desk, fighting the apathy around you, memories of that day are buzzing in your mind. An old pal suggested Tiago, and you have tried to do what he says, but really you think it is all a load of 'civvy tosh'. As he explains about the animal, you are already deciding this will be your last session and you are going to find a shrink in uniform to help.

- Jo, you are a dancer. You have worked for a number of dance companies and had a number of good parts in West End shows. Originally, you are from outside Bristol but now live in London. You have had a string of boyfriends but never really settled down. You were the youngest in the family, with four older brothers. Whenever you get close to a guy, something always gets in the way, and a loyal girlfriend suggested Tiago. You are desperate for kids and do not want to miss the boat. You feel a bit weird in the group. Debbie is always fawning over Tiago even though she is old enough to be his mother and she always directs catty remarks at you. Hugh is completely unreadable but keeps the group happy with his bizarre sense of humour. A number of the exercises have left you feeling a bit lost, but this one sounds right up your street.

- The improvisation will start with Tiago explaining the exercise and then, after giving you all 30 seconds to think of your animal, he invites you up to 'share and triumph'. Afterwards, Tiago tells you there will be a chance to reflect on your findings.

128 STUDENT HOUSE

Student exercise: six-person improvisation

- You are six students, three guys and three girls, that live in a student house in Stoke-on-Trent. You are all third years and are returning to Stoke after your Christmas break. Three of you, the guys, came back last night and had an impromptu party with several members of the university's rugby team, the 'Killer Whales'. The house was trashed after a wrestling competition was held in one of the bedrooms, two windows were broken and a number of mattresses were thrown from upstairs windows and now litter the front garden. The next day, the landlord Mr Baines, who lives round the corner, happened to be walking past his property when he witnessed the aftermath of the party. He knocked on the door and was greeted by a very hungover 'number 8'. The landlord immediately gave one month's notice to vacate the property and threatened to inform the police.

- Gemma, Alison and Tory, you have returned from your holidays to be informed sheepishly by the three boys that you face eviction after the events of the night before. You are less than impressed. Tory and Alison, you were undecided about living with the boys for your third year but Gemma convinced you that it would be fun. You are now sitting in the lounge; a letter has arrived from Mr Baines' solicitor regarding the incident. Tory, you are holding the letter and looking at the three boys – Monty, Den and Spider.

- Monty, you are from Wimbledon and the star full back of the rugby team. You read psychology and care little for academic work, preferring the delights of the university social scene. Nicknamed 'mad bloke' during freshers' week, you have spent the last 2 years living up to the nickname.
- Den, you are a Londoner through and through. You are of Italian and Mauritian heritage and very much the joker of the group. You love nothing more than egging Monty on to get involved in a whole series of daft adventures.
- Spider, you are a six-foot-six Welshman whose ability to consume vast amounts of alcohol is legendary. You study politics and like nothing more than a good debate. You are incredibly clever but lazy and never back down from an argument.
- Tory, you are from the Isle of Man and have lovingly been nicknamed 'Dizzy' by the boys. You are very homely and enjoy your creature comforts. Your room has been thoroughly turned upside down and your bed slept in by a number of the rugby team.
- Alison, you are the serious one of the group. You worked in a merchant bank before coming to university so have a broader understanding of what life is like and you are very keen to do well in your finals. Being the prettiest of the girls, you are often hit on by the boys on nights out; apart from Monty, who you harbour a secret crush on.
- Gemma, you are the hell raiser of the group. Public school-educated, you are a 'posh party girl'. You love living with three outrageous boys and go everywhere the boys and the rugby team goes. You love Tory and Alison but think they need to 'take it easy'; after all, university is meant to be the time of your life.
- The improvisation will start with the three boys sitting on the sofa and Tory and Alison standing before them. Gemma, you are searching for a cigarette.

Notes for the student

This improvisation is very character based, and you will need to choose a practitioner that can help you to delve into the characters. These kinds of improvisations are great to help prepare you for the world of auditioning. It is excellent practice in being given a scenario, given a character and then exploring that character through improvisation.

8 Directing a play

This chapter will take you through the main steps to directing a play and is designed for the student director and the teacher director to use with productions, when directing a play or exploring a play from the director's perspective. This chapter will help you to understand the role of the director and how to structure the process of getting a play up on its feet. Much of this book looks at how we work as the actor, so this chapter will look at how to work from the director's point of view. You may choose to direct your play with a variety of different influences, in which case you can use the exercises in the earlier chapters in the book to help.

I trained as an actor and a director in the Russian tradition of directing, which meant I worked through a series of exercises starting with a very simple still image and then building all the way up to directing a full-length play. This helped me to appreciate how the fine details are everything when directing a play, and how important thinking and walking everything through is when you are directing.

As a director, your job is to tell the audience a story, and all the exercises in this chapter are centred around achieving that objective. If you are ever unsure at any point during the directing process, think about the story you are telling and the message you want to get across to the audience and let that be your guide.

With this chapter on directing following on from seven chapters primarily looking at acting, the focus is on exercises that will structure the director's journey through the play. This chapter will work best when combined with a practitioner of your choice from Chapters 1–4 and Chapter 5 on rehearsing a monologue/duologue.

For teachers, often with the annual show in mind or in some departments the six annual plays/musicals, this chapter will give you a structure to follow to help utilise the time you have available.

129 QUESTIONS AND ANSWERS

Director exercise

AIM

To answer all the difficult questions in the play.

- Having read the play, sit down with a blank sheet of paper.
- Draw up a list of everything you know to be true as it is revealed in the play.
- Write down all the questions you have about the play however irrelevant you think they are.
- Go through them one by one, answering them as you go.
- Start to make decisions as you go.
- Decide on where your play is set (find a map of the local area), what period it is in and what the season is.
- Have a separate sheet of paper for each character and start to write down all you know about that character. Later on, you can pin this to the wall of the rehearsal room and add to it as you go.

Figure 8.1
Discussing the big questions in the play

130 BEFORE AND DURING

Director exercise

> **AIM**
>
> To decide on what happened before the play started and what happens during the play.

- Take the starting point of the play and decide what happens before the events of the play.
- Look at the structure of the play and decide on what happens in between scenes and acts.
- Choose one event that happens before the start of the play and one event in between the scenes or acts of the play.
- Split the cast into two groups and improvise these two moments, and see what you start to find out about the characters and the play.

Notes for the director

Improvising at this early stage of rehearsals helps you to think about the play and the characters on their feet rather than just working round the table. Ask the cast not to play the characters they are likely to play, but rather ones that they are likely not to play so they can start to get a feel for the journey of different characters in the play.

131 SOCIAL, CULTURAL AND HISTORIC INFLUENCES

Director exercise

> **AIM**
>
> To identify the social, cultural and historic influences of the play.

- Split the cast into different groups and each take one of the four areas listed:
    - the writer and his life;
    - the society of the time;

- a historical timeline outlining the main events of the period; and
- the play's genre or category.

• Ask each group to research their area and then feed back to the group.

Notes for the director

This exercise is always an important one, and is about getting into the mind of the writer and understanding the period and genre of the play. If you do this successfully, it will make a number of the exercises later on in this chapter far simpler. Often, finding out about the writer's own life will help you to understand the characters they have created on the page. While working on a play by an Irish writer, Joseph O'Connor, I read up about him and realised that he was the brother of Sinead O'Connor, the singer. I listened to her music and realised it fitted the tempo of the play perfectly!

132 THE DIRECTOR'S COPY

Director exercise

AIM

To create the director's script.

• Copy the script so that each page is on an A4 sheet.
• Make sure there is enough room in the margin to make notes.
• Split the play up into sections, highlighting the main events of the play.
• Label these sections on your script.
• Go through the play, deciding on each character's objectives and actions.

Notes for the director

This exercise can be quite a daunting one. If you are directing a play with ten characters in, then walking the journey of each character to decide what they are thinking and doing throughout the play, it will be quite a task. I would recommend having a clear overview of each character and what each character wants, and then, as you work on each scene, prepare more thoroughly the night before. This puts you in a good position to help the cast find their characters as they go through the rehearsal process. As you get to working on individual scenes, you often have the question, 'What is my character doing in this bit?' or, 'Why am I saying this?' Having already prepared answers for these questions always helps to keep rehearsals flowing.

133 THE READ THROUGH

Director exercise

AIM

To get a complete feel for the whole play.

- Ask the cast to sit around and read the play. Each member of the cast should read a small section of the text before handing over to the next person.
- Split the cast into groups, asking them to come up with the 'play in a nutshell' – one line that best describes what the play is about.

Notes for the director

I always tend to make the read through a light-hearted affair, with the intention to get an understanding of the play rather than starting to perform the play. I would save any auditions or casting until you have read the play and done some initial improvisations. In that way, you give yourself more time to think about who would be right for the different parts.

134 AUDITIONS

Director exercise

AIM

To start to cast the play.

- Before you walk into the audition, have an idea of who you would like to see for what part and then ask them to improvise that part.
- Before they improvise, give the actors a brief synopsis of the plot, given circumstances and what you want them to do.
- Let them improvise a couple of times in a couple of different roles so you can see how they tackle different roles.

Figure 8.2
The key to a good audition is making sure the actors are relaxed so they can then show you what they can do

Notes for the director

Auditions are an opportunity for you to see the suitability of an actor for a part, how an actor takes direction and can start to create a character. It should not really be about the actor's ability to learn lines and then say them cold on the stage with other actors they have not had a chance to rehearse with. I would not give them a script for them to walk around the stage holding, but rather allow them to improvise together so you can start to see them create a character and relationship on stage.

Audition tip

If you are casting a musical, hold acting auditions as well as singing auditions.

135 CHARACTER BIOGRAPHIES

Director exercise

> **AIM**
>
> To start to get the cast to create characters.

- Ask each member of the cast to decide on three key moments in their lives and improvise a short 20-second piece on each.
- The cast then come in and show you their improvisations, allowing them to be a springboard for deciding the further details of their characters' pasts.
- Start to build a picture of how the characters work together. You can ask one character to join another within their improvisations and see how this starts to build relationships.

Figure 8.3
Informal chats with the actors during rehearsals about their characters can often produce interesting discoveries

Notes for the director

This is now a good time to refer to Chapters 1–4 on the practitioners in this book to help flesh out the characters and start to create a style to your piece. As a default, I would go to Chapter 1 on Stanislavski and use those exercises to introduce objectives, actions and start to use active analysis to rehearse the scenes. Or, if you are going for a more epic approach, you can refer to Chapter 2 on Brecht and use the exercises on epization and freeze and gestus. Whichever approach you decide on, use the exercises in Chapters 1–4 on the practitioners to explore and structure the rehearsal process.

136 THE MODEL SHOWING

Director exercise

> **AIM**
>
> To explore your vision of the stage design.

- Create a model of the set you intend to use.
- Design the set and use small figures to represent the cast.
- Show the cast how you intend the set to be and walk them through the play scene by scene.
- Start to think about how you will use lighting within the play as you walk through the scenes.

Director follow-on exercise

- Using masking tape, mark out the set on the floor of the rehearsal room.
- Use the same measurements as the space the actors will perform in.
- Mark out any large furniture that will be on stage for the performance.

Notes for the director

With time limitations, you probably will not be able to produce anything grand, but even a shoebox-style set can help the actors visualise what the eventual staging will be like. If you have someone doing set design, it is a good way of ironing out any miscommunication between the director and the set designer before everything is designed and made for real.

137 THE ESSENCE OF THE PLAY

Director exercise

AIM

To discover the essence of the play.

- Ask each member of the cast to think about what the key message is at the heart of the play.
- Ask them to write it down and then read out all the ideas.
- As a group, merge all the ideas together, coming up with one umbrella label.
- Decide on the label and then the next day come back to the essence of the play again and see if it still works for the whole cast.
- Use the essence to help guide you, as director, in the decisions you make about the play.
- Be open to adapting and updating the play's essence as you go through rehearsal.

Notes for the director

Think of this like your compass that will help steer you in the right direction. For each play, you decide on the compass setting – the play's essence – and then you use it to help guide you through the play. Often, the essence of the play will lie on a subconscious level that may well take a bit of digging to get to.

138 REHEARSING

Director exercise

AIM

To create a clear rehearsal structure.

- Design a rehearsal schedule for the actors to follow with an indication of who should be at each rehearsal.

- Make sure you have enough time to work on each scene at least twice before the first run.
- Schedule in enough runs for the cast to be comfortable with the play.
- Decide on which rehearsal technique you will use – if you choose active analysis (Exercise 17), then make sure you explain fully how you intend to rehearse over the coming weeks.

Notes for the director

Often, when a director has not got a clear strategy for rehearsals, that is when the rehearsals start to go off course. Holding auditions, getting everyone to learn their lines, telling them where to stand and running the play until there are no mistakes is not really a viable option. Think about how you can use techniques such as active analysis or epization to really bring out a directorial style to the piece you are directing.

Directing tip

Guide and steer your actors rather than commanding them. Collaboration is the key.

139 DIRECTING ACTORS

Director exercise

AIM

To get the best from your actors.

- Give notes after each scene has been rehearsed.
- Try not to give too many notes to one actor, but share them out.
- Give homework for the actors to work on for the next rehearsal.
- Be consistent. It is better to think about something overnight rather than making a rash decision.

Notes for the director

On a visit to a local theatre, I sat in on rehearsals. The director was new to directing and giving notes to one of the actors. He gave a series of notes all to do with how the actor should move around the stage. His notes were fairly complex, and the actor was just listening and not jotting them down. The director then said they would run the scene again and did not give the actor with all the notes time to walk through what he had been asked to do. Unsurprisingly, the actor forgot the majority of his lines as he tried to remember where he should be on the stage at a particular point. The director then threw up his arms at the actor's inability to remember his lines and went into a mini tantrum about how the cast have to learn their lines. The director did not allow the actor to orientate to the notes he had been given and walk through the changes. Of course, something was going to drop and it was bound to be the lines. Giving actors time to walk through changes is vital and without it your notes are likely to be forgotten.

Directing tip

If you give an actor a note, make sure he or she writes it down on his or her script.

Figure 8.4
Giving notes

140 A PAUSE

Director exercise

AIM

To create a moment within the play outside of the text.

- Choose a part of the play.
- Design a short moment that can be added that will help the audience to understand the play and the essence of the play.
- Craft the scene so it can drop into the play in harmony with the action of the play.
- Think about how you can use comedy within the pause to add to the atmosphere of the play.
- Think of it like showing the audience a moment or a snapshot from the characters' lives that will help them to understand the characters.

Notes for the director

A play, once directed, will have a number of pauses where action has been added to the play that was not in the initial script, but to the audience will seem as if it was written by the playwright.

141 IMPRESSIVE STAGING

Director exercise

AIM

To create a piece of impressive staging within the play.

- Choose a moment or moments in the play where you can really let your directorial creativity flow.
- Think about how you can create a piece of staging that will add to the audience's enjoyment of the play.
- Refer back to Chapter 3 on Lecoq and Chapter 4 on Berkoff for ideas on how to create impressive moments on stage.

Notes for the director

Part of your job as the director is to create a piece of theatre that the audience will enjoy and be stimulated by. This exercise will help you to sit out of the box of daily or weekly rehearsals and think about designing something breathtaking for the audience. A while ago, I was watching a play that had been written in two acts, with the second act existing 20 years after the first act. The director came up with an impressive and simple way to show the time passing. At the start of the play, he had an actor dressed as a young boy reading a comic on stage. In between the acts, the boy reading the comic came on again and then was replaced by a teenager reading a novel, who was then replaced by an adult reading a newspaper. The change in seasons was projected on the backdrop and, as the changes were stylised, the audience got a better understanding of the play and watched an impressive piece of stage work too.

142 USING SILENCE

Director exercise

> ### AIM
>
> To establish relationships within a play.

- Create a silence within the play where the main characters do not speak.
- Use the silence to let the audience see the relationships between the characters without focusing on the text.
- Think about what you want the audience to understand about your main characters and communicate that through the silence.
- Allow the actors to explore the relationships within the silence.
- Think about how you can tie the silence in with the essence of the play.

Notes for the director

Sometimes the most beautiful moments on stage are in silences when the actors are thinking and doing as the characters, and the relationships become clear to the audience. Think of it like you are creating the 'Oh, I see' moment in the audience's mind. It is often these moments that can shape a performance so the audience fully understand your interpretation of the play. So, if you are trying to communicate a message to the audience, a silence can be the perfect place to do to that.

143 USING COMEDY

Director exercise

AIM

To use comedy effectively within the play.

- Go through the play and identify moments that could be used for comedy.
- Think about how the characters' interactions can create comedy within the play.
- Start to use comedy to heighten the more tragic elements of the play.

Notes for the director

As a director, you can start to think about how you can use comedy to tell the story and to get the message of the play across to the audience. Use comedy to highlight any tragic elements of the piece and to give the audience a chance to watch how others live their lives. By adding a comedic element to a scene, you can often make it more poignant so that it sticks in the mind of the audience.

144 USING MUSIC

Director exercise

AIM

To use music to help tell the story of the play.

- Think about how you can use music throughout your play to support the play and add to the atmosphere of the play.
- Decide on house music for the start of the play as the audience comes in and at the intervals.
- Check to see if there needs to be any character music during the play and make sure it fits with the period of the play you are staging.

- Decide on a scene that will be your music scene where there is no dialogue but action to music.
- Use this like the silence to help tell the story of the play and communicate, as the director, with the audience.

Notes for the director

Music can be very powerful within a play; it helps to set the tone, create atmosphere and identify a period. It may also be used to contrast or distance an audience. Your job is to decide which, and make sure it fulfils its purpose. I directed *One Flew over the Cuckoo's Nest* a number of years ago, and at the start of Act 2 is a scene where all the guys in the ward play basketball. I wanted to have some music that captured the era of the play, while at the same time expressing the patients' enjoyment at playing the game. I used 'Surfin' USA' by The Beach Boys, which, combined with the cast running on in their underwear (in the stage directions), created a very different energy and vibrancy to the scene that would not necessarily have been there without the music.

145 USING SPACE, VOICE AND MOVEMENT

Director exercise

AIM

To ensure the actors are using space, voice and movement.

- Use one rehearsal to watch for how the actors are using space, movement and voice.
- Use the exercises in Chapters 1–4 on the practitioners to help you think about how you can utilise the space and movement on stage.
- Stand at the back of the theatre and check for vocal projection.
- Do this fairly early on so the actors can make sure they fill the space with their voices.
- If you are rehearsing in a small space and transfer to a larger space, make sure you run a vocal projection check before you rehearse and run in the bigger space.

Director follow-on exercise: vocal projection

- Line up the cast in the space they will perform the show.
- Ask each member of the cast to choose a line from the play.
- Tell them to imagine a target on the back wall of the space and, using their voice, they have to hit it and imagine their voice going through the target.
- Imagine the space is full of people and set a volume that will be heard by all the audience.
- As you rehearse and run the play, remind the actors of the projection they need to maintain throughout the performance.

146 DESIGNING THE SET

Director exercise

AIM

To design the set to fit with the play.

- When designing your set, remember that the set is another way of communicating the story of the play to the audience.
- It should fit with the style of the play and your directorial style.
- Keep in mind the essence of the play while you design the set and take the opportunity to walk the cast through the set so they can share in your vision.

147 SPECIAL EFFECTS

Director exercise

AIM

To create special effects within the play.

- Think about how you can use a range of special effects to enhance your play.

- Think how you could use video to project images on the space, or smoke and lighting.
- Aim to use any special effects that enhance the telling of the play's story.

Notes for the director

As many of you will be on a small budget, the opportunity to use special effects may well be quite limited. The use of video is nowadays highly accessible and can create a real effect on the audience. Make sure that any special effects you do have are there to serve the play and that the play does not become about the special effects.

148 THE TECH

Director exercise

AIM

To prepare for a smooth technical run.

- Prepare all light and sound cues before the technical rehearsal.
- Brief your light and sound operatives prior to the rehearsal and give them full cue sheets on the script for each change.
- Make sure you have organised to have all sound cues in order on a CD or digitally ready to play.
- Have the lights positioned before the actors come for the tech.
- Start at the top of the play and run from cue to cue, with the actors in position on stage.
- If you have a complicated sequence of cues, allow the lighting and sound operatives to practise a couple of times so they feel comfortable with the cue changes.

Notes for the director

The tech is all about managing your time, the actors' time and the lighting and sound operatives' time. The more preparation you do in advance, the better the tech will be. You want to avoid having the actors enter the space, and watch the lighting person move the lights around for 2 hours before the cues can be run. Try not to use the tech for acting notes and just run from cue to cue for lights and sound.

149 FINISHING TOUCHES

Director exercise

AIM

To add the finishing touches to the play.

- As you start to put the scenes together, watch for opportunities to link the play together.
- Think about how you can create a visual through line to the play using the characters and structure of the events of the play.
- Relax as you watch the play and, in your notes, add ideas for staging or characterisation that would enhance the enjoyment of the play for the audience.

Notes for the director

The last few days of rehearsals are undoubtedly the most stressful for the director and usually when the director feels vulnerable. It is at this time when you need to sit back, relax and watch the play with an eye to adding the little details that bring the play together. It always helps to have someone sit next to you during the runs so they can offer suggestions on what they see and you can get a fresh opinion on the play.

150 RUNNING THE PLAY

Director exercise

AIM

To run and polish the play.

- Once all the scenes have been rehearsed, run each act of the play from start to finish without stopping. You can run an act and give notes in one session, and then run the next act and give notes in the next session.
- Give notes and feedback on what you saw; allow the actors a day or two to think them over.

- Once you have run the different acts or two halves of the play, put them together and run the whole play.
- Give notes again and then schedule the second and third run.
- Gauge where each actor is, how comfortable they seem with the play as a whole and whether you need to run again before the dress.
- Leave a day before the dress run of the play and then allow the actors time to think about the dress run before the first night.

Notes for the director

When giving notes about a run, try not to give notes such as 'Can you do that bit like you did last night?' The actor then tries to copy the performance they did before rather than creating a new, fresh performance each night. Instead, look back at what you did in rehearsal to create what you liked in the first place and remind the actor of that. Do not worry if the first run is very messy and a lot of the things you told the actors about are not there. Just remind them of what they have forgotten and check to see if it is there in the next run. If an actor is unsure of their lines, just get them to line run the play for cues or ask them to run their lines with another actor.

151 THE FIRST NIGHT

Director exercise

AIM

To manage the first night for the cast.

- On the day of the first performance, bring the cast together an hour before the show.
- Talk them through what you want them to do over the next hour.
- Depending on the demands of the play/musical, you may want to run a movement or vocal warm-up.
- In a quiet space, run a relaxation with the whole cast.
- Give the actors the half hour to prepare themselves for the performance.
- Avoid the temptation to give last-minute notes, and offer each member of the cast encouragement and save the speeches until after the show.

Notes for the director

Recently, I was backstage at a performance, and 15 minutes before curtain up the director was whipping the cast up using an elaborate chant, culminating in a group scream, then group hugs and finally group tears. I am yet to meet a group of young actors that need 'firing up' before going on stage; if anything, they need ways to control and channel their energy into the performance. As a director, you need to give the cast time to prepare themselves mentally and physically and manage their energy levels before they go on stage so they can perform to the best of their abilities. Each actor is different in the run up to opening night, and the best way to deal with that is by making sure that the actors' half hour (the half hour before curtain up) is for the actors, and leave them to do what they have to do.

Afterword

A good few years ago, I was in Moscow with a fellow student (now my wife) on a drama school tour when we bumped into the principal of our school. Walking along, he asked me what I thought of the Russian theatre I had seen so far. I thought for a moment and said I was surprised by the acting. He asked me why and I said that, in the home of Stanislavski, I expected the acting to be less forced and more free. He nodded and we walked on. After a few moments, I asked him why he thought the acting was forced, and he gave me a wry smile and said that, unfortunately, many had taken a path different from the one they could have taken.

Over the years, I have thought about this conversation and how great ideas and practices in theatre can be confused or misinterpreted over time; how practices can be made so theoretical that they no longer are any use in practice; how, across the theatres, schools, colleges and drama schools, students and actors walk around the stage rehearsing, script in hand saying their lines, when this was never the way of working of practitioners such as Stanislavski, Brecht or Lecoq.

In many ways, this is where this book comes from. Hopefully, I, with the help of Annie, Mayumi and Matt, have laid out a simple, practical guide to the key ideas and practices in theatre; a guide that you can pick up and have a clear understanding of how to direct a play, devise a piece of theatre or use Brecht with a text; a guide that will help you to understand theatre how it should be understood: through practice.

Glossary of terms

1 STANISLAVSKI AND THE SYSTEM

action
What we do, as the character, to fulfill our objective.

active analysis
A rehearsal technique where actors analyse a bit of the play 'on their feet'. The actors decide on the main event, an action for each character, then improvise that bit.

active imagination
Seeing things through our character's eyes using the five senses.

bit
A play is divided up into manageable sections or units by the actors and director. A bit starts when there is an event on stage, the character's objectives change or a character enters/exits.

communication
The sending out and receiving of signals between two living beings.

event
Something that happens that affects what you are thinking and doing.

experience
The state where you leave the actor behind and find the character, with everything you do being the product of your character's thoughts and actions.

free body
The desired state for an actor; a body free from tension that can be used to create and experience a role.

germ
The essence or seed of a character.

given circumstance
The situation the character is in within a particular bit of the play.

imagination
The ability to treat fictional circumstances as if they were real.

inner monologue
The thoughts going through a character's mind.

magic if
The question 'what if' that an actor asks himself or herself to trigger the imagination within a given set of circumstances.

objective
What we, as the character, want to achieve within a given set of circumstances.

psychophysical
The combination of what we are thinking and doing that works across the system. What we think and do working together in harmony.

rays
An invisible current that flows between us all the time.

relationships
The thoughts we have about others.

subconscious
The part of the mind that influences our thoughts and actions without us being aware of it.

super objective
The theme of the play; the sum of all the objectives of the characters; what the play is really about. For a character, the super objective is what they want over the course of the play.

tempo-rhythm
Our pace, both mental and physical; the pace of everything around us and everything we do.

through action
What the character does to achieve his or her super objective.

truthful
Acting is truthful when based on a set of given circumstances; you are thinking and doing as the character, imagining actively with a free body and a clear walk through before time.

2 BRECHT

choral work
A piece of theatre rehearsed together with the actors performing in time and to the same rhythm.

class
The position a person holds in society based on his or her wealth, education and upbringing.

de-familiarise
A technique designed to make the audience stop and think about the social effects of the events on stage.

economic
Anything that relates to buying and selling, production and manufacturing of goods and how wealth is achieved.

ensemble
A group of actors performing together.

epic theatre
The term used to describe theatre that uses Brecht's methods and techniques to create theatre with a political, social and economic message.

epization
A rehearsal technique used to create a narrative style of delivery of text.

externalisation
To show thoughts or feelings on the outside using gesture, movement and facial expression.

gestic props
Props that are used by the actor or director to send a message to the audience.

gestus
A gesture that defines the position your character is in within society.

historicization
Setting the events of a play in a different time period to help distance the audience from the given circumstances.

left wing
To follow socialist views.

narrating
The telling of a story.

political
Relates to the government of public affairs and the running of the state.

right wing
To follow conservative views.

social
Concerns the relationship between people and communities within a country.

v-effect
Where the actor attempts to detach himself or herself from becoming lost in the circumstances of the play, while allowing himself or herself to narrate proceedings.

3 LECOQ

action mime
To replay a physical action as close as possible. Also to copy the handling of objects.

attitudes
A series of movements to help go beyond natural gesture.

cartoon mime
Peformed like a silent movie of images.

commedia dell'arte
Masked improvised comedy, originally from Italy.

counter mask
Playing against the emotion a character mask is showing.

dramatic acrobatics
Leaps, jumps, lifts, somersaults and juggling used in performance.

dramatic territories
Key dramatic styles such as comedy and tragedy.

expressive mask
A full character mask with features.

figurative mime
The body used to represent objects.

gaze
In *commedia dell'arte* the end of your nose becomes your eyes.

geo-dramatics
Movement linked to nature to make dramatic landscapes/theatre.

human comedy
Lecoq's style of *commedia dell'arte*.

identification
Finding a character by physical identification with materials and elements.

mimage
A zoom into a character's internal feeling.

mimodynamic
Movement found from colours, words or music.

neutral mask
Used to make your body the focus of expression.

neutral state
When you are in a state of balance before you become a character.

open mime
Central to Lecoq's teaching 'to play at being someone else and summon up illusory presences'.

pantomime
Where gesture alone replaces words; associated with white pantomime/ Pierrot.

storytelling mime
Narrative spoken and used with any of the mime family.

toute bouche
Everything moves.

4 BERKOFF

base pulse
The rhythm and ensemble movement used in choral work.

bouffon
Performance style used by Lecoq drawing on mimicry and the grotesque.

chorus
A non-individual group of performers found in Greek drama who comment together on the dramatic action, both vocally and physically.

cryptos
The Greek meaning of 'hidden'.

grotesque
A fantastic and outrageous element of bouffon.

Japanese Noh theatre
Stylised classical Japanese dance drama using character masks.

Jo-ha-kÿ
A kabuki concept where *jo* is a slow and auspicious beginning, *ha* speeds events up and *kÿ* is a short and satisfying conclusion.

kabuki
A classical Japanese dance drama with elaborate face make-up.

kvetch
Taken from a Yiddish noun and means to complain all the time, usually with humour.

marche sur place
A stylised way of walking on the spot.

mie
A character pose using a heightened physical style.

strip mime
A style used in clowning and pantomime (see Chapter 3 on Lecoq).

total theatre
Performance with equal elements of movement, text, visuals and music.

Notes

1 STANISLAVSKI AND THE SYSTEM

1 Stanislavski, K. (2008) *An Actor's Work* (trans. J. Benedetti), London: Routledge, p. 20.
2 Stanislavski, K. (2008) *An Actor's Work* (trans. J. Benedetti), London: Routledge, p. 84.
3 Stanislavski, K. (2008) *An Actor's Work* (trans. J. Benedetti), London: Routledge, p. 239.
4 Stanislavski, K. (2008) *An Actor's Work* (trans. J. Benedetti), London: Routledge, p. 209.
5 Stanislavski, K. (2008) *An Actor's Work* (trans. J. Benedetti), London: Routledge, p. 473.
6 Stanislavski, K. (2008) *An Actor's Work* (trans. J. Benedetti), London: Routledge, p. 476.

2 BRECHT

1 Willett, J. (1977) *The Theatre of Bertolt Brecht*, London: Methuen Drama, p. 170.
2 Brecht, B. (1960) *The Caucasian Chalk Circle*, London: Methuen Drama, p. 136.
3 Brecht, B. (1964) *Brecht on Theatre: The Development of an Aesthetic*, London: Methuen Drama, p. 136.
4 Brecht, B. (1960) *The Caucasian Chalk Circle*, London: Methuen Drama, p. 31.
5 Thomson, P. (2010) *Actor Training* (2nd Edition, ed. A. Hodge), London: Routledge, p. 125.
6 Brecht, B. (1960) *The Caucasian Chalk Circle*, London: Methuen Drama, pp. 12, 13.
7 Brecht, B. (1964) *Brecht on Theatre: The Development of an Aesthetic*, London: Methuen Drama, p. 180.

3 LECOQ

1 Lecoq, J. (2000) *Belle Ile en Mar in The Moving Body*, London: Methuen Drama, p. 187.
2 Lecoq, J. (2000) *The Moving Body*, London: Methuen Drama, p. ix.
3 Lecoq, J. (2000) *The Moving Body*, London: Methuen Drama, p. 69.
4 Lecoq, J. (2000) *The Moving Body*, London: Methuen Drama, p. 71.
5 Lecoq, J. (2000) *The Moving Body*, London: Methuen Drama, p. 73.
6 Lecoq, J. (2000) *The Moving Body*, London: Methuen Drama, p. 81.
7 Lecoq, J. (2000) *The Moving Body*, London: Methuen Drama, p. 94.
8 Lecoq, J. (2000) *The Moving Body*, London: Methuen Drama, p. 22.
9 Berkoff, S. (1994) *Greek: The Collected Plays Volume One*, London: Faber and Faber.
10 McBurney, S. (2003) *Complicitie's Plays One*, London: Methuen.
11 Petterle, D., Monaghan, N. and Heimann, C. (2010) *100*, London: Nick Hern Books.
12 Rudkin, J. (1994) *Commedia dell'arte: An Actor's Handbook*, London: Routledge.
13 Lecoq, J. (2000) *The Moving Body*, London: Methuen Drama, p. 82.
14 Neruda, P. (1972) *The Captain's Verses* (trans. D. D. Walsh), New York: New Direction Publications Corporation.
15 Anonymous (2006) *The Voyages of Sinbad*, London: Penguin Epics.
16 McBurney, S. (2003) *Complicitie's Plays One*, London: Methuen.
17 Teale, P. (2005) *Brontë*, London: Nick Hern Books.
18 Lecoq, J. (2000) *The Moving Body*, London: Methuen Drama, p. 47.
19 Rudkin, J. (1994) *Commedia dell'arte: An Actor's Handbook*, London: Routledge.
20 Lecoq, J. (2000) *The Moving Body*, London: Methuen Drama, p. 104.
21 Lecoq, J. (2000) *The Moving Body*, London: Methuen Drama, p. 105.
22 Lecoq, J. (2000) *The Moving Body*, London: Methuen Drama, p. 106.

4 BERKOFF

1 Berkoff, S. (2009) 'An Interview', *The Independent*, 29 February.
2 Berkoff, S. (2010) *Diary of a Juvenile Delinquent*, London: Arum Press.
3 Berkoff, S. (1994) *Dog and Tell Tale Heart: The Collected Plays Volume Two*, London: Faber and Faber.
4 Flying Fox in *Heavenly Sword* (PlayStation 3, 2007).
5 Lust, A. (2000) *Post-Modern Mime from Greek Mimes to Marcel Marceau and Beyond*, Lanham, MD: Scarecrow Press.
6 Berkoff, S. (1995) *Meditations on Metamorphosis*, London: Faber and Faber, p. 142.
7 Lecoq, J. (2000) *The Moving Body*, London: Methuen, p. 139.
8 Barrault, J. L. (1935) Staging of *As I Lay Dying*, France.
9 Lecoq, J. (2000) *The Moving Body*, London: Methuen, p. 84.
10 Lecoq, J. (2000) *The Moving Body*, London: Methuen, p. 124.

11 Berkoff, S. (1994) *Greek: The Collected Plays Volume One*, London: Faber and Faber.

12 The Killers (2008) 'Human', *Day & Age*, Island Records.

13 Berkoff, S. (1994) *Greek: The Collected Plays Volume One*, London: Faber and Faber.

14 Berkoff, S. (1995) *Meditations on Metamorphosis*, London: Faber and Faber, p. 31.

15 Berkoff, S. (1995) *Meditations on Metamorphosis*, London: Faber and Faber, p. 55.

16 Berkoff, S. (1988) *Metamorphosis*, London: Amber Lane Press, p. 83.

17 Philip Glass (1986) 'Colourbox', *The Official Colourbox World Cup Theme*, 4AD.

18 Berkoff, S. (1995) *Meditations on Metamorphosis*, London: Faber and Faber, p. 54

19 Berkoff, S. (1988) *The Trial*, London: Amber Lane Press, Introduction.

20 Berkoff, S. (1995) *Meditations on Metamorphosis*, London: Faber and Faber, p. 49

21 Berkoff, S. (2010) 'A Provokation', Australian lecture.

22 Berkoff, S. (2010) 'An interview', *The Independent*, 29 February.

Further reading

STANISLAVSKI

Carnicke, S. M. (2009) *Stanislavsky in Focus* (2nd Edition), London: Routledge.

Knebel, M. (2012) *Action Analysis*, London: Routledge.

O'Brien, N. (2011) *Stanislavski in Practice*, London: Routledge.

Stanislavski, K. (2009) *An Actor's Work*, London: Routledge.

BRECHT

Brecht, B. (1964) *Brecht on Theatre* (ed. and trans. J. Willett), London: Methuen.

Mumford, M. (2009) *Bertolt Brecht: Performance Practitioner Series*, London: Routledge.

LECOQ

Brook, P. (1968) *The Empty Space*, Harmondsworth: Pelican.

Graham, S. and Hoggett, S. (2009) *Frantic Assembly Book of Devising Theatre*, London: Routledge.

Leabhart, T. (1989) *Modern and Post War Mime*, London: Macmillan.

Lecoq, J. (2000) *The Moving Body*, London: Methuen Drama.

Mitchell, T. (1984) *Dario Fo People's Court Jester*, London: Methuen.

Rudkin, J. (1994) *Commedia dell'arte: An Actor's Handbook*, London: Routledge.

BERKOFF

Berkoff, S. (1995) *Meditations on Metamorphosis*, London: Faber and Faber.

Berkoff, S. (2010) *Diary of a Juvenile Delinquent*, London: Arum Press.

MONOLOGUES AND DUOLOGUES

Earley, M. and Keil, P. (1992) *The Classical Monologue: Men*, London: Methuen.

Earley, M. and Keil, P. (1992) *The Classical Monologue: Women*, London: Methuen.

Earley, M. and Keil, P. (1993) *The Modern Monologue: Men*, London: Methuen.

Earley, M. and Keil, P. (1993) *The Modern Monologue: Women*, London: Methuen.

Harvey, A. (2002) *Methuen Book of Duologues for Young Actors*, London: Methuen.

Salt, C. (2003) *Methuen Drama Book of Contemporary Monologues: Men*, London: Methuen.

Salt, C. (2003) *Methuen Drama Book of Contemporary Monologues: Women*, London: Methuen.

DIRECTING

Mitchell, K. (2009) *The Director's Craft*, London: Routledge.

Index of terms and exercises